Droupadi Murmu

'The biography is a realistic portrayal of the life and times of Madam Murmu. Precisely yet generously the book deals with details of her path to success through ups and downs… It will remain an inspiration for generations.'

—**Ganeshi Lal**
Governor of Odisha

'A well-researched, close look at one of the most inspiring lives in contemporary India. Intrepid journalist Kasturi Ray traces the personal and political journey of President Droupadi Murmu, from humble beginnings to public life during an epochal period in the nation's history, earning a reputation for integrity and idealism, firm but with a gentle demeanour. The challenges she had to overcome along the way make this book well worth reading, and it is captivatingly told.'

—**Baijayant 'Jay' Panda**
National vice president of the BJP, columnist and author

'A remarkable book about a remarkable woman who, despite all odds, rose to great heights to take the highest office in the land, from a village that had no electricity, roads, or schools. Ms Droupadi Murmu is an inspiration not only to our tribal communities but, rather, to each one of us, and this biography brings this fact out like no other biography can. A must-read.'

—**Anand Ranganathan**
Author and scientist

'The story of Droupadi Murmu deserved to be told, not just as India's first tribal woman president, but as a beacon of the new India that is emerging, breaking the shackles of its colonial past. Kasturi Ray has done a great job in putting together a non-hagiographical account through in-depth research and interviews.'

—**Sandip Ghose**
Author and political commentator

Droupadi Murmu

FROM TRIBAL HINTERLANDS TO RAISINA HILL

KASTURI RAY

RUPA

First published by
Rupa Publications India Pvt. Ltd 2023
7/16, Ansari Road, Daryaganj
New Delhi 110002

Sales Centres:
Prayagraj Bengaluru Chennai
Hyderabad Jaipur Kathmandu
Kolkata Mumbai

Copyright © Kasturi Ray 2023

The views and opinions expressed in this book are the author's own and the facts are as reported by her which have been verified to the extent possible, and the publishers are not in any way liable for the same.

All rights reserved.
No part of this publication may be reproduced, transmitted, or stored in a retrieval system, in any form or by any means, electronic, mechanical, photocopying, recording or otherwise, without the prior permission of the publisher.

P-ISBN: 978-93-5702-200-2
E-ISBN: 978-93-5702-198-2

First impression 2023

10 9 8 7 6 5 4 3 2 1

The moral right of the author has been asserted.

Printed in India

This book is sold subject to the condition that it shall not, by way of trade or otherwise, be lent, resold, hired out, or otherwise circulated, without the publisher's prior consent, in any form of binding or cover other than that in which it is published.

To Papa and Bapa

Contents

Foreword	*ix*
Prologue: The Die Is Cast	*xiii*
Introduction	1
1. The Fragrance of Tulsi Leaves: Childhood	34
2. An Emancipation of Sorts: College and First Job	64
3. A Wife and Teacher: Marriage, Children and People	79
4. The One with No Peer: On-Ground Legislation	99
5. Warm Clothes in the Winter, an Umbrella in the Rain: Grief and Spirituality	137
6. True Stateswoman: Jharkhand Governor	158
7. Fifteenth President, Her Excellency	189
Acknowledgements	238
Index	239

Foreword

'You must understand the whole of life, not just one part of it. That is why you must read, that is why you must look at the skies, why you must sing, dance and write poems, and suffer, and understand, for all that is life.'

—Jidu Krishnamurti

To understand the basic tenets of life, one reads, values, appreciates and imbibes. We look up to people who not only create an identity of their own but leave an indelible mark on the pages of history.

President of India Droupadi Murmu is one such personality, whose inspirational life has been discussed in bits and pieces ever since she was elevated to the position. The author Kasturi Ray, in her first attempt at life narrative, has tried to unravel Murmu's life from her childhood to the present day through poignant storytelling. She takes the readers through a mosaic of struggles and successes Murmu has laid on her way to the topmost position of the country.

Born in a Santali-dominated village in the remote Mayurbhanj district of Odisha, Murmu began her education in the local primary school and continued up to Class 5. Among the many firsts she carved in life, stepping out of the village to pursue higher education was noteworthy, given the tribal background she hailed from and the then prevailing social norms.

Right from holding a job in a government department to becoming a school teacher, and from then beginning her political journey, the book takes us through the uphill path Murmu took to reach Raisina Hill.

Murmu contested the first election of her life in 1997 for Rairangpur Notified Area Council (NAC) as a Bharatiya Janata Party (BJP) candidate and won. Since she was one of them, the tribals and the underprivileged found a voice in her. She also won the Assembly elections in 2000 as a BJP candidate and went on to become a minister in the Biju Janata Dal (BJD)–BJP alliance government in Odisha. Her term as the commerce and transport minister was highly appreciated. She was awarded the Pandit Nilakantha Award in 2007 in the Odisha Assembly for the best Member of Legislative Assembly (MLA) of the year.

Her efforts as head of the home department standing committee, which submitted a hard-hitting report to the government to bring about corrective measures for the prisons and prisoners during her term as an MLA, are praiseworthy.

Despite losing her loved ones, including both her sons and husband, her zeal to be with the people of her constituency showed the indomitable spirit of a woman, mother and wife. Her spiritual journey to rediscover herself and bounce back to stand with the people remains exemplary.

In 2015, she became the governor of Jharkhand, and in the six years she was in office, she was known for her firmness in decision-making without any political interference. Apart from upholding her constitutional rights, she revolutionized the education scenario in the state and was also known for her refusal to give approval to the Santhal Pargana Tenancy Act, 1949, and Chota Nagpur Tenancy Act, 1908, terming them anti-tribal.

Now, as she leads the country as the first citizen, her commitment to the cause of the people has only gotten magnified.

In the seventy-fifth year of the country's independence, when Murmu's presidentship has raised hopes of billions of citizens in the country, her life comes alive with the turn of every page in the book.

—**Kiran Bedi**
Indian Police Service (Rtd) and
Former Lt Governor, Puducherry

Prologue: The Die Is Cast

'Main, Droupadi Murmu, Ishwar ki shapath leti hoon ki main shraddhapurwak Bharat ke Rashtrapati ke pad ka karya palan karungi, tatha apni puri yogyata se samvidhan aur vidhi ka parirakshan, sanrakshan aur pratirakshan karungi. Aur main Bharat ki janata ki seva aur kalyan me nirat rahungi.'[1]

—Droupadi Murmu, President of India

At a time when India was celebrating seventy-five years of Independence, a voice from a remote tribal village in Odisha resonated across the central hall and corridors of Parliament—the temple of the largest democracy in the world. In a packed auditorium, Droupadi Murmu was administered the oath of office of the fifteenth President by Chief Justice of India N.V. Ramana on 25 July 2022. Draped in a white handloom sari with a saffron and green border, reflecting the colours of the national flag, Murmu

---

[1] 'I, A.B., do swear in the name of God/solemnly affirm that I will faithfully execute the office of President (or discharge the functions of the President) of India and will to the best of my ability preserve, protect and defend the Constitution and the law and that I will devote myself to the service and well-being of the people of India.' 'Oath or Affirmation by the President', *Constitution of India*, https://bit.ly/40D2yHO. Accessed on 7 February 2023.

took the oath of office in Hindi and soon after addressed the Parliament House in her maiden speech, which was followed by a twenty-one gun salute.

And the rest is history.

Introduction

On 21 June 2022, the otherwise quiet, narrow lanes and by-lanes of Uparbeda, Droupadi Murmu's native village, tucked miles away from the district headquarters of Baripada and 260 km from Odisha's capital Bhubaneswar, woke up to a renaissance. And it was the same day when even Rairangpur town—14 km from Uparbeda and 85 km from Baripada, which gave Murmu, the people's representative and humane politician, an identity—was reborn.

As the news of the presidential nomination began trickling in, the woman of the moment was in Rairangpur. Unfortunately, Murmu and her family were not able to watch the news because of a power cut. Yet the indications were apparent. The sense of serendipity was palpable. What had happened six years back when she was chosen the governor of Jharkhand was being replayed, albeit in a larger and grander way.

Murmu looked calm from the outside. She seemed unaffected, in a state of poise, while everyone else was waiting for the euphoric moment outside her double-storeyed house situated in ward number 2 of Baidaposi, on Mahuldiha Road in Rairangpur.

As if gathering pieces of her life, she took some time to adjust to the fact that she was being chosen to be the first tribal woman president of the largest democracy by the National Democratic Alliance (NDA) led by the Bharatiya Janata Party (BJP) as well as the first to be born after Independence, even though there was no official confirmation yet. There were tears in her eyes, even as she kept full control over her emotions.

Murmu's house was a dwelling like any other political leader's. Painted in pastel green, it was an ordinary residence, with the sun shining on its walls on a sunny late afternoon. Over the next few hours, people slowly started gathering nearby, and the house turned into a fort with a security blanket all around. A posse of police personnel from the Odisha police and Central Reserve Police Force (CRPF) cordoned off the place, imposing restrictions on the people who wanted to meet Murmu. By then, television channels had started broadcasting the news.

As people gathered, she invited everyone in, met them and spoke to them. Not a frequent mobile phone user, she had kept hers away and probably missed many calls, including the most important one of her life. But as her daughter Itishree's phone was constantly ringing, Murmu managed to respond to a few.

Her silence eclipsed words even at the height of excitement. She felt she was being recognized and rewarded for the years of hard work, service and devotion to the soil and work she had done.[1] The official confirmation was still awaited.

The hour of reckoning finally came when her former officer on special duty for a brief stint at Jharkhand and currently a medicine store owner in Rairangpur, Bikash

---

[1] 'Daughter Itishree Shares on Mother Droupadi Murmu Chosen as Presidential Candidate' (Video in Odia), YouTube, https://bit.ly/3ESsHcv. Accessed on 3 March 2023.

Chandra Mohanto, came running to Murmu's house with his phone in hand. He had apparently received a call from the Prime Minister's Office (PMO) and was asked to connect with Murmu. Taken by surprise and unable to fathom the urgency, he lowered his store's shutter and rushed to Murmu's house to connect her to the PMO.

She had not realized by then that she had missed the most important call of her life on her phone. Mohanto handed over his phone to Murmu with Prime Minister (PM) Narendra Modi on the other end—they spoke. She knew she was the NDA's choice as the presidential candidate.

At a loss for words, Murmu expressed her doubt if she would be able to shoulder the responsibility as expected and Modi assured her that she could. 'The Constitution will guide and show you the right path.... Prime Minister told me that the way you groomed Jharkhand while being Governor of the State, I am confident that you will also be able to fulfil this responsibility quite efficiently,' she said much later, during a meeting of legislators and parliamentarians in Ranchi.[2]

CONGRATULATIONS AND SUPPORT

After her candidature was publicly announced by the BJP national president J.P. Nadda on the evening of 21 June 2022, she was assigned Z+ security. 'For the first time, preference has been given to a woman tribal candidate. We announce Droupadi Murmu as NDA's candidate for the

---

[2]Ranjan, Mukesh, 'Droupadi Murmu Gets Emotional, Says She Is Connected to Jharkhand by Blood,' *The New Indian Express*, 4 July 2022, https://bit.ly/3YfM99Y. Accessed on 3 March 2023.

upcoming Presidential elections,' Nadda declared in New Delhi.[3]

Murmu was asked to go to Delhi the next morning for nomination formalities. For her, 21 June was a red-letter day. Spending time with family after celebrating her sixty-third birthday on 20 June at Rairangpur, she had not realized the sixty-fourth year of her life would bring with it the responsibility of becoming the president of India. Overwhelmed, she did not get the time to even speak to her family members. Itishree, who has been a constant companion of Murmu and for whom her mother is an ideal, was with her in Rairangpur at this time. She shared that no one in the family had imagined this birthday gift for Murmu. After the confirmation came from Nadda, the phones did not stop buzzing. 'I could not speak to her properly as she left for Bhubaneswar the next day. But I knew that once she has been named by the party and if she became the president, she would not remain only my mother. She would become the country's,' she said. 'We were all so overwhelmed with so much love and affection showered on my mother.'[4]

Itishree, who has seen her mother brave many challenges and personal tragedies in her life, felt that it was her years of hard work, dedication and struggle that brought her to this position. 'Starting out from a place that

---

[3] 'BJP Names Former Jharkhand Governor Droupadi Murmu as Its Presidential Candidate,' *Hindustan Times*, 21 June 2022, https://bit.ly/3X4QH2o. Accessed on 7 February 2023.

[4] 'Daughter Itishree Shares on Mother Droupadi Murmu Chosen as Presidential Candidate' (Video in Odia), YouTube, https://bit.ly/3ESsHcv. Accessed on 3 March 2023; 'Presidential Poll: Draupadi Murmu To File Nomination Today, Discussion With Her Daughter Itishree,' YouTube, https://bit.ly/3T9rJ1g. Accessed on 13 March 2023.

did not have a fair-weather road, electricity or even basic facilities, my mother's journey from the tribal hinterlands to Raisina Hill is nothing less than inspiring,' she said.[5]

Life was changing. Though it was late at night, the line of people, political friends, opponents, supporters, relatives and neighbours wanting to meet Murmu never shortened. Camera flashes kept lighting up the room as every visitor wanted a photograph with her. The framed photographs of her near and dear ones hung around the walls were probably drawing her attention, reminding her that they were with her in her success and happiness.

Soon, echoes of celebration reverberated across the district from every locality. Drums, clarinets and tribal tunes started playing while men and women danced all night. Tribal dances were organized by various communities in her native village and in-laws' village in Pahadpur, while pots of *handia* (a drink made with fermented rice) were gulped down by the villagers.

By then, livestreaming of news had begun, and broadcasting vans of regional channels had lined up in front of the house. In one of her interviews at that moment, Murmu politely expressed her gratitude to everyone for being with her and said, 'I am surprised as well as delighted. As a tribal woman from the remote Mayurbhanj district, I had not thought of becoming the candidate for the top post. The NDA government's decision to nominate a tribal woman for the top post is a reflection of the BJP's slogan of *sabka saath, sabka vikas, sabka vishwas* [Together, for

---

[5]'Presidential Election 2022 Draupadi Murmu ki Beti Itishree Murmu ne Batai Unke Struggle ki Kahani,' YouTube, http://bit.ly/3Le5Mwh. Accessed on 13 March 2023.

everyone's growth, with everyone's trust[6]]. I would not want to say anything else now. I am happy to see you all here for having come and met me with good wishes.'[7]

As the night passed and the number of visitors grew, the BJP members and close associates suggested she retire for the day because she had to leave for Delhi the next morning. Though her conscience wanted her to stay awake and meet whoever came by, she had to call it a day.[8]

Murmu woke up, as she usually would, at 3.00 a.m. the next morning, just after an hour of sleep. She started the day as usual with meditation and yoga and went to visit a few places of worship before leaving for Bhubaneswar, from where she was to catch a flight to New Delhi the next day, 23 June. Getting into a vehicle amid tight security, she went to a Shiva temple in the town, sought blessings and swept the floors as she customarily did. She also went to Jaher, a place of worship for the Santal, the tribe to which she belongs. She offered her prayers there and stopped by other temples too to pay obeisance.

She then bid adieu to Rairangpur as she started on a new journey. After seven hours on the road, she reached Odisha's capital, which was replete with large posters, hoardings and banners congratulating her on the nomination. She stayed at the Mahanadi Coalfields Limited

---

[6]'PM Modi Reiterates "Sabka Saath, Sabka Vikas, Sabka Vishwas" Motto at UN ECOSOC Virtual Meet,' *The Statesman*, 17 July 2020, http://bit.ly/3FkMm4W. Accessed on 13 March 2023.
[7]'First Reaction of Draupadi Murmu after BJP Announced Her Name as NDA Presidential Candidate,' YouTube, https://bit.ly/3yfYYGQ. Accessed on 6 March 2023.
[8]As stated by the people who were there—BJP member Nabin Kumar Ram and Member of Legislative Assembly (MLA) Naba Majhi—during their interviews.

guest house for the night. Even at the guest house, there were a large number of people from various walks of life waiting outside with bouquets and good wishes. The rush seemed to never end.

Early next morning, she was greeted by some of her school friends, family and acquaintances, many of whom she had wished to meet. 'I did not want to break the protocol but was there at the guest house to see her off,' said Dangi Murmu, a schoolmate who came to see her off.[9]

On Murmu's request, a former general manager at the Bank of India, Ishwar Chandra Mishra, who has been her family friend for years (Mishra and Murmu's husband Shyam Charan Murmu were colleagues in the Bank of India), reached the guest house. Though Mishra was reluctant because of the protocol hassles and security issues, she assured him that he would be let in. 'I have called you here for a purpose. Please offer prayers to Lord Jagannath on my behalf as I am rushing to Delhi for this important assignment. I know only you can do this for me,' was what Mishra recollected her having told him. 'I was overwhelmed to hear that she wanted me to do the puja on her behalf at Srimandir. I immediately said I will,' he narrated.[10]

Once all was set, she left for the Biju Patnaik International Airport, with people standing on either side of the road waving at her. The airport had filled literally to the brim, right from the parking lot to the waiting lounge for visitors.

---

[9]All quotes by Dangi Murmu are from an interview conducted by the author on 20 December 2022.
[10]All quotes by Ishwar Chandra Mishra are from an interview conducted by the author on 6 December 2022.

The sounds of blowing conches, the rhythm of drums and folk songs were floating from all directions. The tribal people of the area had gathered in their traditional attire and were celebrating in groups outside the airport. Members of political parties were also seen singing and dancing, enjoying the moment. Flanked by top leaders of the BJP, including Bhubaneswar Member of Parliament (MP) Aparajita Sarangi as well as the BJP Odisha's General Secretary Lekhashree Samantasinghar and State President Samir Mohanty, Murmu went inside the airport and was whisked away to the airliner.

In a brief statement issued before her departure for the national capital, she said, 'I thank all and seek cooperation from everyone for the presidential election. I will meet all voters (lawmakers) and seek their support before July 18.'[11]

Odisha Chief Minister (CM) Naveen Patnaik, who supported Murmu's candidature in principle, took to Twitter to congratulate the NDA's nominee: 'I was delighted when Hon'ble PM @narendramodiji discussed this with me. It is indeed a proud moment for people of Odisha.'[12] Patnaik, who was then in the Vatican City, further added, 'I am sure [she] will set a shining example for women empowerment in the country.'[13] He also sought everyone's support for the 'daughter of the soil' Murmu. He said her

---

[11]'Murmu Leaves for Delhi, Seeks Cooperation from All for Presidential Polls,' *The Indian Express*, 23 June 2022, https://bit.ly/3lguMbg. Accessed on 8 February 2023.
[12]@Naveen_Odisha, *Twitter*, 21 June 2022, 10.49 p.m., https://bit.ly/3JhcekG. Accessed on 6 March 2023.
[13]@Naveen_Odisha, *Twitter*, 21 June 2022, 10.50 p.m., https://bit.ly/3JgjeOL. Accessed on 6 March 2023.

Introduction 9

nomination as the ruling NDA's presidential candidate is a proud moment for the state and appealed to all MPs and MLAs from Odisha to unitedly vote for her and ensure her victory in the presidential polls.

Biju Janata Dal (BJD) leader and MP Sasmit Patra termed Murmu's candidature as an important event that would be written in the pages of Odisha's history. He stated that CM Patnaik has been personally overseeing the process in Odisha and has appealed to the Congress leader and leader of Opposition (LoP) Narasingha Mishra to vote for her.[14]

IN DELHI

After reaching Delhi, Murmu met PM Modi before her nomination for the election was filed. In a tweet, he said that her presidential nomination 'has been appreciated across India by all sections of society. Her understanding of grassroots problems and vision for India's development is outstanding'.[15]

Not only the BJD but the Jharkhand Mukti Morcha (JMM) also lent support to Murmu. In a one-page letter to party MLAs, JMM president Shibu Soren said, 'This is the first time post independence that a tribal woman would be getting honour to become president. After long deliberations, the party has decided to support Murmu in the election. All party legislators, MPs are directed to

---

[14]"CM Naveen Patnaik Reaches Out To All MLAs For Support To Droupadi Murmu: Sasmit Patra,' YouTube, http://bit.ly/3yfzWYk. Accessed on 6 March 2023.
[15]@narendramodi, *Twitter*, 23 June 2022, 2.24 p.m., https://bit.ly/3Zn3z5V. Accessed on 6 March 2023.

vote in favour of Murmu on July 18.'[16] Besides, Janata Dal (United) (JD[U]) chief Nitish Kumar, Andhra CM and Yuvajana, Shramika, Rythu Congress Party (YSRCP) chief Jagan Mohan, Bahujan Samaj Party (BSP) chief Mayawati and Shiv Sena chief Uddhav Thackeray agreed to go with the BJP's choice for the presidential election that was slated for 18 July.

On 24 June 2022, the day of the nomination filing, Murmu paid floral tributes to Mahatma Gandhi, Dr Bhimrao Ambedkar and Birsa Munda and then reached Parliament, clad in a pristine white sari. Prime Minister Modi, Home Minister Amit Shah, central ministers, CMs of all the BJP-ruled states, Meghalaya CM Conrad Sangma, Nagaland CM Neiphiu Rio, MPs and ministers from Odisha and other top leaders were present during the filing formalities. Besides, members of other NDA parties, including Anupriya Patel of the Apna Dal, Rajiv Ranjan Singh of the JD(U) (then an ally) and All India Anna Dravida Munnetra Kazhagam (AIADMK) leaders M. Thambidurai and O. Panneerselvam, were also among those present to extend support.

Of the four sets of nomination papers required to be submitted, PM Modi proposed the first, while the second set was proposed by J.P. Nadda along with CMs of BJP-ruled states. The third set was signed by MLAs and MPs from Himachal Pradesh and Haryana while the fourth set had MLAs and MPs from Gujarat as proposers. The uniqueness of this election was the representation of tribal MLAs and MPs in most sets of nomination papers.

---

[16]'Shibu Soren's JMM Now Backs Droupadi Murmu for President,' *Hindustan Times*, 14 July 2022, https://bit.ly/3XCSvQk. Accessed on 17 February 2023.

The nomination papers were submitted to the Secretary General of the Rajya Sabha P.C. Mody, appointed as the returning officer by the Election Commission of India (ECI).

After verification of the documents in the presence of all proposers at the Sansad Bhavan library, the secretary general proceeded with the formalities and PM Modi finally signed the papers, completing the process.

Murmu had earlier interacted with Opposition leaders from the Congress, the All India Trinamool Congress (TMC) and the Nationalist Congress Party (NCP), seeking support. The presidential nominee spoke to the then Congress interim president Sonia Gandhi, West Bengal CM Mamata Banerjee and NCP chief Sharad Pawar. Banerjee wished her luck, though she did not commit to supporting her.

Pitted against Murmu was Opposition candidate Yashwant Sinha, who filed his papers on 27 June. Chosen by the Congress, Samajwadi Party (SP), National Conference, NCP, All India Majlis-e-Ittehadul Muslimeen (AIMIM), Rashtriya Janata Dal (RJD), TMC, Communist Party of India (CPI), Communist Party of India (Marxist) (CPI-M) and All India United Democratic Front (AIUDF), Sinha, a bureaucrat-turned-politician, had joined active politics by becoming a member of the Janata Dal in 1984. Later, he joined the BJP and became its national spokesperson in June 1996. After being elected thrice to the Lok Sabha as a BJP candidate from Hazaribagh, he went on to become the finance minister from March 1998 to July 2002. In 2018, he quit the BJP and has been a staunch critic of Narendra Modi's government ever since. In 2021, he joined the TMC ahead of the 2021 West Bengal Assembly Election. He was chosen by the Opposition parties to fight the 2022 Presidential Election against Murmu.

The election was certainly historic because of the NDA's decision to field a candidate from the marginalized section, an Adivasi, for the post of the president. The NDA, led by Atal Bihari Vajpayee and Narendra Modi, has been known for its experimental choice in candidates for the top position in the country. Dr A.P.J. Abdul Kalam was chosen during NDA-I under Vajpayee, the NDA-II chose Ram Nath Kovind, a Dalit person, as the president, while NDA-III selected Droupadi Murmu from the Scheduled Tribe (ST) community. Her nomination was seen as a part of the Modi government's policy of giving voice to people from the fringes who have remained unrepresented so far.

HITTING CAMPAIGN MODE

The presidential election was scheduled on 18 July and the result was to be out on 21 July.

As per the Chief Election Commissioner Rajiv Kumar:

> No political party can issue a whip to its members. The President of India is elected indirectly by the votes cast by an electoral college, comprising 776 members of Parliament which includes members of Lok Sabha and Rajya Sabha and the members of legislative assemblies. A total of 4,809 votes will be cast. The value of the votes of the members of assemblies combined is 543,231 and that of the MPs is 543,200, equalling a value of 1,086,431. The nominated members of both the houses or legislative assemblies are not eligible to participate in the election.[17]

---

[17]'Announcement of Election to the Office of President of India 2022,' YouTube, https://bit.ly/3ZZW2tv. Accessed on 13 March 2023.

Ahead of the elections, Murmu was given an elaborate itinerary to visit states and seek support from all political parties. A fourteen-member committee was set up to coordinate the travel. Jal Shakti Minister Gajendra Singh Shekhawat led the team at all the places.

As her whirlwind tour of states began, Murmu met Hemant Soren, the CM of Jharkhand and other BJP MPs and MLAs. During her tour to Meghalaya, she met MPs and MLAs of the ruling Meghalaya Democratic Alliance. The BJP, with two MLAs in the House of sixty, is a constituent of the National People's Party-led coalition in Meghalaya. In Tamil Nadu, she had a meeting with the alliance party representatives; she was accompanied by Minister of State for Information and Broadcasting Dr L. Murugan, BJP Tamil Nadu President K. Annamalai and MLA Nainar Nagendran, among others. The AIADMK's support was conveyed by its leaders of both the warring factions and former CMs K. Palaniswami and O. Panneerselvam. She also went to West Bengal and met BJP MPs and MLAs and visited Lucknow to interact with the BJP legislators there.

Campaigning in her home state of Odisha on 8 July was special, as a grand reception was accorded to her at the airport, with the BJP legislator Kusum Tete and Bhubaneswar MP Aparajita Sarangi dancing and playing cymbals as congratulatory gestures. The BJP state president Samir Mohanty, BJD vice-president Debi Prasad Mishra and many senior leaders of the BJP and the BJD were present too.

Tribal women dressed in traditional attire performed Ghoda and Bagha *nacha* (horse and tiger dance) to musical tunes on the streets leading to the airport. Groups of *kirtan* [devotional songs] singers performed on those roads as well. A lot of people had gathered to catch a glimpse of the Odia presidential candidate. 'She is the pride of #Odisha. Reiterate my appeal to all members to ensure every vote in her favour,' CM Patnaik tweeted.[18]

Organizational secretary of the BJD Pranab Prakash Das also met the leader of the Congress Legislature Party (CLP) Narasingha Mishra at his chamber in the Assembly while a team of BJD leaders met Sarat Pattanayak, president of the Odisha Pradesh Congress Committee (OPCC), seeking support for Murmu.

Union education and skill development minister and BJP leader Dharmendra Pradhan appealed to the Congress members to support her candidature. However, the members maintained that they had already taken a stand, as the party had its own candidate. Mishra said that the presidential election was not a matter of caste, creed or locality and that the party would stand by its ideological commitment.[19]

In the 147-member Odisha Assembly, the BJD had 112 members, while the BJP had twenty-two. The Congress had nine MLAs while the CPI-M had one member. The House had only one Independent member, and two members were expelled from the BJD.

Chief Minister Patnaik, who directly handled the presidential election, was present at the State Assembly entrance to welcome Murmu. He reiterated that she deserved unanimous support of all MPs and MLAs of

---

[18] @Naveen_Odisha, *Twitter*, 5 July 2022, 7.33 p.m., https://bit.ly/3mrZhf5. Accessed on 6 March 2023.
[19] 'Presidential Polls: Odisha CM Naveen Patnaik Reaches Out to All MLAs for Support to Droupadi Murmu,' *The New Indian Express*, 6 July 2022, https://bit.ly/3EHNPSB. Accessed on 27 February 2023.

the state and called upon them to cast their votes in her favour.[20]

Not many are aware that Murmu has been tying a rakhi to Patnaik every year since at least 2000. She said that the CM's support of her was a gift of a brother to a sister. 'As per our Jagannath tradition, I tie the rakhi to him as Devi Subhadra does to Lord Jagannath. And he unconditionally gifted me the support to take on the highest office of the democracy,' she stated in the Odisha Assembly when she went to meet and interact with the MLAs and MPs from Odisha ahead of the election.[21] Murmu said she has worked with many of the BJD MLAs as colleagues after being elected to the State Assembly. All of them are like brothers and sisters to her. 'I may not know some of them personally if they became members of the House after I left, but technology has brought all of us closer. I seek support from all,' she stated.[22]

She met the BJP MPs and MLAs at the State Guest House and had lunch with the CM at Naveen Nivas along with Gajendra Singh Shekhawat and Puri MP Pinaki Mishra before leaving the state. Sources at the CM's residence revealed that on that day, Odia delicacies such as *baigan bhaja, alu bharta* and *badi chura* were served with rice and dal for lunch in honour of Murmu and other ministers.

On 18 July 2022—the election day—PM Modi was among the first to cast his vote in Parliament followed by

---

[20]@Naveen_Odisha, *Twitter*, 22 June 2022, 5.14 p.m., https://bit.ly/41HsSkN. Accessed on 6 March 2023.
[21]'CM Naveen Patnaik Kept Rakhi Promise, Will Be Indebted to Him for Support: Droupadi Murmu,' YouTube, http://bit.ly/3SQL8nz. Accessed on 6 March 2023.
[22]Ibid.

Nadda. Amit Shah, Sonia Gandhi and Rahul Gandhi also cast their votes. Many ailing leaders came to vote as well despite being unwell: Ex-PM Manmohan Singh and SP founder (late) Mulayam Singh Yadav arrived in Parliament on wheelchairs; Pradipta Kumar Naik, BJP leader and LoP in the Odisha Assembly, reached with an oxygen cylinder directly from the hospital where he had been admitted due to post-Covid complications. The election saw leaders cutting across party lines going that extra mile to ensure their votes counted.

Voting also took place in state assemblies across the country. As per the ECI, eleven states—Chhattisgarh, Goa, Gujarat, Himachal Pradesh, Kerala, Karnataka, Madhya Pradesh, Manipur, Mizoram, Sikkim and Tamil Nadu—as well as the union territory of Puducherry recorded 100 per cent polling.[23]

The Parliament House recorded 98.90 per cent voter turnout at the end of the polling for the presidential election. Addressing the media after the voting, Returning Officer P.C. Mody said that of the 736 electors permitted by the ECI to vote (comprising 727 MPs and nine MLAs), 728 (719 MPs and nine MLAs) had cast their votes.[24]

In Maharashtra, 283 out of 287 MLAs took part in the voting process held at the Maharashtra Vidhan Bhavan in south Mumbai. The BJP legislator Laxman Jagtap, who was unwell; Shiv Sena MLA Mahendra Dalvi, a member

---

[23] 'Presidential Polls: Over 99% Turnout, 100 pc Voting in 11 States,' *The Tribune*, 18 July 2022, https://bit.ly/3YZIGxa. Accessed on 17 February 2023.

[24] 'Presidential Polls: Over 99% of 4,796 Electors Cast Votes; 100% Turnout in 10 States, 1 UT,' *The Indian Express*, 18 July 2022, https://bit.ly/3KJRoLU. Accessed on 27 February 2023.

of the outfit led by CM Eknath Shinde, and jailed NCP lawmakers Anil Deshmukh and Nawab Malik did not vote.

In Punjab, Shiromani Akali Dal (SAD) MLA Manpreet Singh Ayali boycotted the presidential poll, alleging that the NDA's farm laws of 2020 were against the interest of his state so he would not support their candidate. Moreover, the SAD, he alleged, had not taken his opinion on the issue of supporting the NDA candidate.

CROSS-VOTING

Cross-voting took place during the elections, which became evident after the results came out. Cross-voting is a process where voters exercise their franchise for a candidate based on their own choice, going against the party's decision. In all, cross-voting took place in seventeen states. Within those states, 126 MLAs and seventeen MPs went against their party lines to vote for Murmu.[25] The biggest instance of cross-voting in her favour was reported in Assam, where twenty-six non-BJP lawmakers voted for her.

There could be many reasons behind cross-voting, but first and most importantly, the trend indicated the unanimity of leaders in cutting across party lines to support Murmu and wanting her as the president. Second, it indicated cracks within the Opposition alliances. The most common reason of cross-voting is believed to be Murmu's clean image and her performance in the past as the constitutional head of Jharkhand.

---

[25]'Presidential Election: What Cross-Voting from Opposition Members In Favour Of Droupadi Murmu Means,' *Outlook*, 22 July 2022, https://bit.ly/3kuhBn0. Accessed on 27 February 2023.

Only one MLA of the NCP in the Gujarat Assembly, Kandhal Jadeja, voted for Murmu. This came as a surprise because the NCP is an ally of the Congress-led United Progressive Alliance (UPA) in Gujarat. Speaking to media persons after casting his vote, Jadeja said that he voted for the BJP candidate, but he was soon asked by Gujarat NCP president Jayant Patel for an explanation.[26] Jharkhand NCP MLA Kamlesh Singh also announced that he had voted for the NDA presidential nominee. He said that his conscience made him vote in her favour.[27]

According to BJP sources, around 125 MLAs from different assemblies cross-voted in Murmu's support. 'Assam, Jharkhand and Madhya Pradesh assemblies witnessed a significant number of Opposition MLAs voting for the BJP-led NDA's candidate plus around twenty-two MLAs in Assam and twenty in Madhya Pradesh assemblies are likely to have cross-voted. Six Opposition MLAs each from Bihar and Chhattisgarh, four from Goa and 10 from Gujarat may also have voted for Murmu,' the Press Trust of India reported.[28] The report further stated that Murmu received maximum votes from Uttar Pradesh and Maharashtra while Sinha got most support from West Bengal and Tamil Nadu. Additionally, all MLAs from Andhra Pradesh, where the ruling YSRCP as well as the

---

[26] 'Presidential Polls: Party Seeks Explanation after NCP MLA Votes for Murmu,' *The Indian Express*, 19 July 2022, http://bit.ly/3JfscdI. Accessed on 13 March 2023.

[27] '"Went by Conscience": NCP, Congress MLAs Vote for Droupadi Murmu in Presidential Poll,' *Deccan Herald*, 18 July 2022, http://bit.ly/3l9nVRi. Accessed on 13 March 2023.

[28] 'Cross-voting from Opposition Members Helped Boost Droupadi Murmu's Tally,' *Mint*, 21 July 2022, http://bit.ly/3LiewkQ. Accessed on 13 March 2023.

Opposition Telugu Desam Party (TDP) had pledged support to Murmu, voted for her. She also received all the votes from Sikkim and Nagaland. On the other hand, Sinha swept all votes from Kerala MLAs, as the state-ruling Left and the Opposition Congress both supported him.

Immediately after the results were declared, the BJP's Amit Malviya tweeted, '2 TMC MPs and 1 MLA cross voted. Vote of 2 TMC MPs and 4 MLAs declared invalid. Mamata Banerjee, self appointed fulcrum of opposition unity, failed to prevail over her own legislators. On the other hand, despite intimidation, all BJP WB legislators backed Smt Droupadi Murmu...'[29]

Assam CM Himanta Biswa Sarma also tweeted, 'Smt Droupadi Murmu polled 104 votes compared to NDA's original strength of 79 in the 126 member Assam Assembly. 2 absent. My heartfelt gratitude to the people of Assam for reposing their faith in the NDA's Presidential candidate & wholeheartedly joining this historic moment.'[30]

It is noteworthy that one of Odisha Congress's MLA Mohammed Moquim voted for the BJP's Murmu against the party's decision to vote for Yashwant Sinha. It was Moquim who confirmed this soon after casting vote for Murmu. He stated:

> In Presidential elections, there is no whip from the parties. Moreover, it should be a decision of the conscience to vote for a candidate of choice. Murmu was undoubtedly my choice and my state's choice. It was a matter of 4.5 crore Odias who wished to see the

---
[29]@amitmalviya, *Twitter*, 22 July 2022, 12.15.a.m., https://bit.ly/3F5zuPZ. Accessed on 6 March 2023.
[30]@himantabiswa, *Twitter*, 21 July 2022, 8.11 p.m., https://bit.ly/3YjgJQ9. Accessed on 6 March 2023.

daughter of the soil to be positioned as the President of the country.[31]

He was later issued a show-cause notice by the OPCC President Pattanayak. But Moquim clarified that it was not because of voting for Murmu but the statements he made to the media after voting, which the senior leadership felt were anti-party. The OPCC accused him of being involved in carrying out propaganda against the party and its programmes. 'You are deliberately acting and carrying on propaganda against the programmes and decisions of the Congress. You are frequently addressing the electronic media, deliberately acting in a way calculated to lower the prestige of the Congress. You are carrying out propaganda against the Congress and its office-bearers,' the notice read.[32]

In the seventy-fifth year of India's independence, according to Moquim, having a woman from Odisha, the first from a tribal community, to be voted as the president was an exceptional opportunity. He reasoned:

> I voted for Murmuji because for me, my soil comes first and the party later. There has been precedence in many states in India. Indira Gandhi had appealed to the party MLAs and MPs to exercise franchise as per conscience. There is no party whip. Now too, everyone should vote independently. I can answer my

---

[31] Quote from interviews conducted by the author on 20 January 2023 and 10 March 2023

[32] Mohapatra, Debabrata, 'Odisha Congress Serves MLA Mohammed Moquim Notice for Voting in Favour of NDA Presidential Candidate Droupadi Murmu,' *The Times of India*, 23 July 2022, https://bit.ly/3lNkT54. Accessed on 20 February 2023.

party people in a closed door discussion and not in front of the media.[33]

He cited the example of Pratibha Patil, who was voted by the Shiv Sena, going against the decision taken by the alliance, as well as the example of Pranab Mukherjee, who had Mamata Banerjee's support. Moquim added that Hemant Soren voted for Murmu too, despite being in the JMM because of his affinity for the Adivasi Santals.

In Uttar Pradesh, in an interesting turn of events, Shivpal Singh Yadav said that his letter to the SP lawmakers led to cross-voting. It came to the fore that twelve SP lawmakers had cross-voted for Murmu. Meanwhile, it was understood that her chances of winning maximum votes in Maharashtra were higher after the political developments around that time. The Shiv Sena faction led by Eknath Shinde toppled the Uddhav Thackeray-led Maha Vikas Aghadi government. Previously, the same Shiv Sena had pledged its support to Sinha, but soon after the government was toppled, both Uddhav and Eknath supported Murmu.

Moreover, Mamata Banerjee took all Opposition parties by surprise when she said that she would have lent all support to Murmu had the NDA declared her name ahead of the Opposition deciding on Yashwant Sinha. Her soft stance in the case of Murmu was critiqued by Congress leader Adhir Ranjan Choudhury in the Lok Sabha, who said that she buckled under the BJP's pressure. 'It was Didi who chose Sinha for the Opposition candidate and forced others to follow her. She taking a u-turn indicates that Modi must

---

[33]Barik, Satyasundar, 'Cross-voting in Presidential Election, Odisha Congress MLA Votes for NDA Candidate Droupadi Murmu,' *The Hindu*, 18 July 2022, https://bit.ly/3Sc2g6Y. Accessed on 20 February 2023.

have pressurised her as she is in good rapport with him,' Choudhary said.[34] He also went on to say that while other Opposition members, like Bharat Rashtra Samithi (BRS) in Telangana and the CPI-M in Kerala, wholeheartedly supported Sinha, the TMC was found to be lacking in its commitment.[35]

RESULTS

Counting of votes was scheduled for 21 July. Post elections, the ECI stated in a press note: 'Polling for election to the office of President of India, which is the highest elected office in the country, concluded successfully in free, fair and transparent manner at the Parliament House and in each of the 30 places of poll in State Legislative Assemblies including Legislative Assembly of NCT of Delhi and UT of Puducherry.'[36]

After the end of the counting process that continued for more than ten hours, Returning Officer Mody declared that the value of votes Murmu got was 676,803 against Sinha's 380,177.[37]

---

[34]'Adhir Ranjan Slams Mamata, Says She Is Doing Everything to Weaken Opposition,' *The Economic Times*, 16 December 2021, https://bit.ly/3J9kqUc. Accessed on 3 March 2023; 'Droupadi Murmu Could Have Been Consensus Candidate, Says Mamata Banerjee,' *The Hindustan Times*, 14 July 2022, https://bit.ly/41HMaGM. Accessed on 3 March 2023.
[35]The BRS used to be known as the Telangana Rashtra Samithi (TRS). Its name was changed on 5 October 2022.
[36]'Polling for Presidential Elections 2022 Held Peacefully Today,' *Press Information Bureau*, 18 July 2022, https://bit.ly/416VBPB. Accessed on 20 February 2023.
[37]It is important to note that the result of the presidential election in India is determined by the value of the votes, not number of votes. The value assigned to the votes of MLAs is different from that of MPs'; it also

It was the day of the daughter of India, a moment of reawakening for India as Droupadi Murmu was elected to the office of President of India. A new dawn, filled with hopes and aspirations of a new India, rose. Born after Independence—the youngest thus far—an Adivasi woman had been elected as the first citizen of the world's largest democracy, to be known henceforth as Her Excellency. In his congratulatory message, PM Modi tweeted, 'India scripts history. At a time when 1.3 billion Indians are celebrating Azadi Ka Amrit Mahotsav, a daughter of India hailing from a tribal community born in a remote part of eastern India has been elected our President! Congratulations to Smt. Droupadi Murmu Ji on this feat.'[38]

Celebrations began everywhere. Sambit Patra, the BJP spokesperson, posted pictures dancing with Adivasis and locals in Odisha's Jasuapur, near Pipili. West Bengal BJP leader Suvendu Adhikari took part in the revelry in Kolkata. Nagaland BJP vice president Benjamin Yepthomi uploaded visuals of a rally he was a part of in support of Murmu. Andhra Pradesh, Gujarat, Karnataka and almost all parts of the country rejoiced. Irrespective of party affiliations, people celebrated the day as the victory of democracy. This included tribal communities, political parties and other well-wishers.

---

varies according to states. While the value of the vote of an MP from either the Lok Sabha or Rajya Sabha is 700, the value is different for each State Assembly depending on the state's population. For instance, the value of a vote of an MLA from Mizoram or Arunachal is eight, while the same for an MLA from Uttar Pradesh is 208. The total value of votes of MPs and those of MLAs is roughly same. For a detailed understanding of the vote calculation process, please refer to https://bit.ly/3IyMoY3. Accessed on 6 March 2023.

[38] @narendramodi, *Twitter*, 21 July 2022, 8.21 p.m., https://bit.ly/3ZMI3XU. Accessed on 7 March 2023.

'A daughter of Odisha, a tribal girl, a sister was addressing the nation. I feel lucky to see history being written,' Odisha CM Patnaik said in a tweet. He had also stated in an editorial in Odia ('E Matira Kanya' [Daughter of the Soil]) that Murmu is the symbol of aspiration and hope for crores of women in the country and signifies women's empowerment; it was published across all mainstream Odia newspapers.

Indeed, India had made history. People showered their wishes on the president. From the Dalai Lama to former President Ram Nath Kovind, from Amit Shah to Punjab CM Bhagwant Mann, congratulatory messages kept pouring in. Several Opposition leaders, including Sonia Gandhi, Mamata Banerjee and Sharad Pawar, also congratulated Murmu.

The Union education and skill development minister Dharmendra Pradhan said that there could not have been a better time for electing a president from a marginalized community. A day after the result was declared, he stated:

> When we are celebrating 75 years of Independence in the form of Azadi Ka Amrit Mahotsav and laying the roadmap for the coming years, President Murmu's election is a victory of the democracy. It is the win of every citizen of the country... On behalf of Odisha, I would like to thank PM Modi, NDA leadership, and all the parties of India who believe in democracy for voting for Murmu. For all Odias, it is a matter of pride even more that for the first time, a daughter, mother and sister of Odisha is elected to lead the country as President.[39]

---

[39] 'Dharmendra Pradhan Calls President Droupadi Murmu's Win a "Victory of Democracy",' YouTube, http://bit.ly/3STuLOl. Accessed on 7 March 2023.

DRUMS, DANCING AND CELEBRATIONS

At Uparbeda, people came out of their houses in hordes and burst into merrymaking. The celebrations continued for days. They swung to traditional folk dances and broke into a chorus of folk songs. Once again, the tribal households saw handia flowing freely as a mark of celebration. The road to Murmu's village was chock-a-block with people, which included television crews, journalists, well-wishers and relatives. 'There were people who did not even understand what becoming the president means. Everyone just knew that the girl from their own village has done something unthinkable and that made them dance in joy,' said former JMM legislator Prahlad Purty.[40]

Separate groups of men and women performed the Santali dance in circular and semi-circular formations. While women were seen dancing with their arms interlocked, the men in dhoti and turban played drums and other percussion instruments. In cluster formations, the dancers performed from where the village began to where it ended with no holds barred. There were many who joined the celebration in the form of typical Santali victory songs.

'It was a festival from morning to evening and none went for their daily chores of agriculture works or even goat rearing,' Purty added. The otherwise silent and peaceful village of Uparbeda was reborn, he said. Never will it be described again as nondescript. People, normally busy at this time of the year in cultivation works and poultry rearing, were seen living in the moment. Purty stated:

---

[40] All quotes by Prahlad Purty are from an interview conducted by the author on 13 November 2022.

The village has been the birthplace of prominent leaders, but someone becoming the president was unprecedented. For the residents, the elections in the past had not much significance, as most leaders did not pay heed to their needs. Only Didi (Murmu) was the one who changed the prospects during her ministerial tenure. So when the same person got to the topmost position, the villagers knew they could expect better days ahead.

The wife of Murmu's nephew Bhagat, Dulari Tudu, was at a loss for words to explain the celebrations. Dulari, who stays in Murmu's native house with her family, said, 'For two whole days, we did not get a minute to even talk to *Peesi* (father's sister, meaning Murmu).'[41]

She did not get an opportunity to spend much time with Murmu, as by the time she wed into the family, Murmu was married and living in Pahadpur and Bhubaneswar. However, Dulari remembered Murmu's drive for social improvement—she encouraged girls from her village to become educated whenever she visited her native village. Dulari reminisced:

> Along with her family, she started staying at Rairangpur mostly after her husband was posted in the town. But because she was born here, the day of nomination and election saw chaos all around. None wanted to stop dancing. Many asked us what changes we were looking forward to as the president belongs to this village. But I honestly said to all of them that nothing matters

---

[41]All quotes by Dulari Tudu are from an interview conducted by the author on 13 November 2022.

now. Our own daughter of the soil has become the President and that is so gratifying and satisfying that we don't need anything else.

It was a feeling of pride that a daughter from the family has become the president, Dulari claimed.

The people from the villages in the vicinity, who were equally ecstatic at the news, said in unison, 'This is how we pay our respects to someone who achieves something exceptional from our community.'[42] They too were making merry and exchanging sweets.

Rairangpur, the town in which Murmu spent a significant portion of her life, was not to be left behind in terms of celebrations. Large LED screens and television sets were blaring the news of Murmu's election as president and celebrations across the country at full volume. The town was dotted with posters and paintings on the walls and the district was celebrating with gusto. The smaller hamlets between Uparbeda and Rairangpur were also celebrating. 'We prepared 20,000 laddus and put up 100 banners congratulating Murmu,' local BJP members said.[43]

The trader community in Rairangpur lowered their shops' shutters and joined the celebrations by preparing sweets for distribution among at least 50,000 people. Gourab Agarwal, an active member of the Marwari community in Rairangpur, whose mother Kanta Devi Agarwal was the councillor from ward number 6 when Murmu was transport and commerce minister between 2000 and 2004, spoke about how celebrations took place on the streets. It was

---

[42] All quotes by Dulari Tudu are from an interview conducted by the author on 13 November 2022
[43] Quote from an interview conducted by the author on 27 December 2022

not Murmu's victory; it was as if the town had won. Every shop in Rairangpur, every small and big gathering was rejoicing. Everyone remembered Murmu fondly for the way she had mingled with them. A very sociable person, she would stand by each family through good and bad occasions. Gourab remembered her gracing his marriage ceremony and clicking pictures with him. On the day of Murmu's nomination and winning the presidential election, Gourab said that the community made 40,000 laddus and distributed them at random on the streets. The other trading communities also prepared thousands of sweets as a mark of celebration. He narrated:

> There was time when we had a serious law and order issue concerning the Hanuman Vatika land. There was a lathi charge by the police, but I remember she was the one in the first line standing with all of us. A complete people's person, she was a commoner like all of us. She never had any airs because she was a minister or MLA. We are all so happy that Murmu Madam has finally written her name on the presidential palace.[44]

Murmu's house in Rairangpur became the cynosure of all eyes. Amid police security, the place was brimming with people. The residents and BJP members from the town continued gathering there for celebrations for hours, though the woman of the hour was miles away. The house gained a special status in a matter of days. Even now, people visiting the town make it a point to go the house to just see where the current president spent most of her time, says Sarita Mandal, a college student from Rairangpur.

---

[44]Quote from an interview conducted by the author 27 December 2022

Taranisen Tudu, Murmu's brother who has been by her side for a long time, was ecstatic. He said, 'I am overjoyed that my sister, a tribal woman, has been elected as the president. She has struggled a lot since her childhood. This is an inspiration for everybody.'[45] Taranisen and his wife Sakramani mostly stayed wherever Murmu did and accompanied her to Jharkhand when she became the governor of the state.

'We are happy because one of us has gone on to become the president,' said a group of women in Salia Sahi, an Adivasi-dominated slum in Bhubaneswar. 'She is an Adivasi like us and a woman who is not an English medium educated person; she had a humble academic background, she fought all challenges in life and today it's our victory. Now our girls and boys can dream big.'[46]

The Odisha Assembly in the state capital, which was in session, went into a frenzy. Legislators distributed sweets among themselves, and many tribal MLAs were also seen dancing on the streets.

Rabindra Patnaik, president of the school management committee of Sri Aurobindo Integral Education and Research Centre in Rairangpur, where Murmu taught for several years, said that the celebration was not just for a day. Patnaik and Murmu's husband were posted in the Rairangpur branch of the Bank of India. Happy that he had inducted her into the school as a teacher, he stated:

> The students and staff started the celebrations from the day she was selected and continued for a month. We

---

[45] '"Defined By Her Simplicity", Droupadi Murmu's Proud Brother Tells NDTV,' YouTube, https://bit.ly/3YHfdYa. Accessed on 13 March 2023
[46] Quote from interview with the author conducted on 28 December 2022

had feasting, dances and performances, besides study circles in the month-long celebrations. The students are inspired to the hilt because she mentioned the school in her maiden speech after [the] oath. She said her turning point in life was getting into teaching at the school. We wish she could come to the school here in Rairangpur.... Someone known as a banker's wife got a different identity as a teacher way back in the 1990s, and now her identity will give all of us associated with her a new identity.[47]

Similarly, students of Rama Devi Women's University (earlier Rama Devi Women's College under Utkal University) wore traditional tribal clothes and jewellery and danced the whole day to celebrate Murmu's elevation to the position of the president. They organized rallies in the campus and were joined in the celebrations by senior BJP leader Surama Padhy, a former student of the varsity and Murmu's junior in the college.

Utkal University students, too, celebrated the day on the campus while Murmu's school in Bhubaneswar, Government Girls High School, Unit 2, was thronged by many just for the sake of getting a glimpse of the alma mater of the new president. Her friends from school gathered there for a few moments to relive the old days and remembered her as a student and their friend.

Though Murmu spent only a little more than six years in Jharkhand, the people in the state continue to remember and appreciate her work. If Odisha celebrated her elevation to the top post in the best way possible, Jharkhand was

---

[47]All quotes by Rabindra Patnaik are from interviews conducted by the author on 29 December 2022, 13 January 2023 and 21 January 2023.

no less. As soon as she won the election, Ranchi, her *karmabhoomi* (place of work), too celebrated with equal gusto and burst crackers, besides indulging in revelry and distributing sweets.

Murmu had created an identity for herself as a constitutional head of Jharkhand who had a mind of her own. In states like Jharkhand, where tribal rights had been neglected for years, she exercised her powers to practise the Constitution in letter and spirit.

SOME NEGATIVE VOICES

Amid the elation, there were some who were critical of Murmu's election. They felt she was only a symbol of empowerment of the marginalized and believed that the atrocities against the Scheduled Caste (SC) and ST communities would still continue. This had happened previously as well, when Ram Nath Kovind had been criticized by senior CPI-M leader from Odisha Janardan Pati, who stated that no visible change could be felt for the Dalit community during Kovind's presidentship, even though he belonged to that community.[48]

Expressing his sense of uncertainty, Akshya Kumar, the national coordinator of the Naba Nirman Krushak Sangathan, a farmers' group in Odisha, cited the tribal unrest due to protests against bauxite mining in Koraput. 'As far as a token of symbolism is concerned, I am happy to see her in that position. But if the symbol is not translated into a vision, strategy and implementation, just becoming

---

[48]Senapati, Ashis, 'Droupadi Murmu's Village in Odisha Celebrates Her Win with Fanfare,' *DownToEarth*, https://bit.ly/3YoWOPS. Accessed on 3 March 2023.

the president will not affect the community in general. I did not see any change when she was the governor also,' Kumar says.[49]

More surprisingly, the Opposition's candidate, Yashwant Sinha, also did not deter from labelling Murmu as a rubber-stamp president. Sinha reacted after Murmu's election and asserted, 'I believe today we do not need a silent president who gets elected to the post but does not discharge constitutional obligations. The president has the right to give suggestions to the government but if he or she is a puppet in the hands of the prime minister, then he or she will not do it.'[50] He also said that the battle is not between two individuals but between two ideologies.[51]

Meanwhile, the Congress party, via the Twitter handle of the Puducherry Congress, tagged Murmu as a 'dummy'. After a massive backlash, these tweets were deleted.

Akhil Giri, a TMC leader, also stirred up the hornet's nest through his comments on Murmu. On 11 November 2022 at Nandigram, Giri had made denigrating remarks about the president during a public meeting. Following this, the BJP appealed for him to be sacked and arrested. It also drew the attention of the National Commission for Women, which sought action against him in the form of a written apology. The BJP also stated that Mamata Banerjee and the TMC were anti-tribal.[52]

---

[49] Quote from an interview conducted by the author on 11 March 2023.
[50] 'Country Does Not Need "Silent" President at This Juncture, Says Yashwant Sinha,' *The Economic Times*, 1 July 2022, http://bit.ly/3TdIyZb. Accessed on 15 March 2023.
[51] 'Country Should Not Have 'Rubber-Stamp President'; Fight Is Ideological: Yashwant Sinha,' *The Wire*, 22 June 2022, http://bit.ly/3TiLZhc. Accessed on 15 March 2023.
[52] '"Have You Looked at Her Face": TMC Minister Makes Derogatory

Introduction

Ahead of the presidential elections, even the RJD leader Tejashwi Yadav took a potshot at Murmu. 'We don't want a statue in the Rashtrapati Bhavan,' he said. 'Everyone must have heard Yashwant Sinha; has anyone heard about the NDA candidate, has anyone heard her speaking?'[53]

As President Murmu takes on her mantle, millions of people await to see her perform her constitutional duties and usher in a new era for the people on the fringes. She has exemplified tremendous grit and determination in bringing about reforms and development of the marginalized communities. Her appointment at the crucial juncture of 'Azadi Ka Amrit Kaal [golden era]' is believed to be a crucial step in paving the way for national development and witnessing India play a pivotal role in leading the world.

As per PM Modi's clarion call for building an *Atmanirbhar* [self-reliant] Bharat during the Amrit Kaal, which stresses on removing slave mentality, stabilizing sectoral imbalances and ushering in a self-reliant India, Murmu could be just the right person, the first citizen of the country, to lead the 1.4 billion people to perform such duties to the maximum.

Remarks about President Murmu, Shamelessly Tries to Defend It Later,' *OpIndia*, 13 November 2022, https://bit.ly/3KfY0BA. Accessed on 20 February 2023.

[53]'Tejashwi Yadav Insults Droupadi Murmu Ahead of Presidential Election; Calls Her 'Statue President' Republic World,' YouTube, http://bit.ly/41Vaxke. Accessed on 9 March2023.

1
The Fragrance of Tulsi Leaves: Childhood

Around 260 km from the state capital of Odisha, which is about a five-hour road journey, mostly through lush green forests, lies Uparbeda village in Kusumi block of Mayurbhanj district. Surrounded by mountain ranges and the Budharana forest that separates Odisha and Jharkhand, Uparbeda is a clean, green village with well-laid tar roads, cleanly painted mud, concrete and clay houses and serene environs.

From the national highway passing through Jashipur square between Baripada and Keonjhar towns, Uparbeda can be reached by taking a turn from Kaduani Chhak. A long bridge from it leads the way through many smaller hamlets to the village. The bridge was built when Droupadi Murmu was the transport and commerce minister in the BJD–BJP alliance in Odisha during 2000–04. Until then, a temporary bridge built with pipes was the only way to reach the main road. During her college days, Murmu used to take the same bridge to cross the river and catch a bus from Kaduani Chhak to reach Bhubaneswar.

THE SANTAL TRADITION

Uparbeda is a Santal-dominated village. Santal people in Odisha are mostly inhabitants of Mayurbhanj, Keonjhar and Balasore districts with a total population of 894,764 as per the 2011 Census. They speak the Santali language. Santal is one of the sixty-two STs found in India. It is considered to be one of the most populous tribal communities, predominantly situated in Mayurbhanj, Odisha, and also in neighbouring states like Jharkhand, West Bengal, Bihar and Assam.[1] The representation of Santali people in the state and central government service is far better than other tribespeople.

The word 'Santal' is derived from two words in Santali: 'santa' meaning calm and peaceful and 'ala' meaning men. The Santals are nomads who used to move in search of agricultural land. Gradually, they settled down in the Chota Nagpur plateau. Towards the end of the eighteenth century, they migrated to the Santal Parganas of Bihar and then they came to Odisha. The Santalis have their own script called 'Ol Chiki', created by Pandit Raghunath Murmu. Apart from settled cultivation, they also migrate and work as agricultural labour as well as in mines and industries. They are involved in silkworm rearing to manufacture Tassar silk, carpentry and rearing bullocks, goats, pigs and fowl for sale and domestic consumption.

The Santal villages are surrounded by agricultural fields, pastures, ponds, graveyards and a common place of worship known as Jaher Era or simply Jaher. Located at the outskirts of the villages, the Jaher is the sacred grove comprising

---

[1] For a full list of the tribes, please see: 'Tribes of Odisha', *Odisha State Tribal Museum*, https://bit.ly/3KNe7a1. Accessed on 3 March 2023.

Sal trees, within which their deities are believed to reside. The villages are not densely populated, and the Santals live in clusters of fifteen to twenty houses at most.

Every surname that is a part of the Santal tribe indicates a specific role in the tribe. 'Murmus are *pujak*s [servitors] while Tudus are singers and dancers,' said Jyotirmayee Tudu, an assistant professor of public administration in Utkal University, Odisha.[2]

The primary occupation of the Santal people is settled agriculture. Both men and women are engaged in this pursuit. As an egalitarian society, women and men work equally. Tudu explains, 'Daughters are considered assets for a Santali family. But the Santali society does not easily agree to marry off their daughters to men outside their tribe. They fear that their cultural practices and traditions will end if she goes to a different tribe because the cultural practices of all tribes are conflicting.'

When tribes migrate to urban areas, cultural assimilation is natural. But cultural preservation should be an individual choice that is not imposed. 'I chose an urban lifestyle and do not continue with the typical rituals associated with our tribe,' Tudu said, explaining the way of life for the Santals.

She also explains how marriages in Santal families are not lavish but low scale. 'There is no concept of dowry in our marriages. Rather, the groom's family gives something to the bride's family during the wedding. Moreover, any ritual of a Santali family is about collective celebration. Neighbours and families in the vicinity unite and contribute

---

[2]All quotes by Jyotirmayee Tudu are from an interview conducted by the author on 10 December 2022.

rice, pulses, vegetables, etc. for the marriage. Earlier, even for housing, most people in a hamlet used to lend their labour and complete the work. But winds of change have made things different. Now all households have good money and they can manage their expenses,' she said, explaining the Santal way of life.

Rice is the Santals' staple food. Usually, they eat *pakhala* (watered rice) with boiled greens and vegetable curry. Handia is a very popular drink among the Santals. The women usually prepare it and, during festivals and rituals, both men and women love to drink it.

Against the backdrop of mountain ranges, the houses in every tribal hamlet are aesthetically painted with natural colours made from clay soil—brick red, blue and yellow. Available in the vicinity, the clay, once fetched from the mountain ranges, can be made into various hues with the right combination of soil and natural dye colours.

Most Santals are adept at these skills and paint their mud walls with many motifs—fish and trees being the common ones. However, geometrical shapes are the recurrent themes in most dwelling units, only some of which are concrete. The houses are sparklingly clean, with cow dung paste evenly spread all around the courtyards. Most houses have a dedicated space for paddy storage as well as goat and poultry sheds. As part of an agrarian village, residents either have large tracts of agricultural fields, which are their only means of sustenance, or are adept at goat and poultry rearing. Men and women participate equally in every agricultural activity while the children go to school these days. In fact, while women shoulder equal work in the fields as men, they also do the household chores, including cooking and cleaning.

There is a constant flow of people from Odisha to Jharkhand and vice versa. They commute on a daily basis for work through the lush green forests of the region. People from both the states have shared traditions and culture. The tribals of Uparbeda have a rich tradition of singing and dancing, praying at Jahers and forest conservation. Though Uparbeda has been home to indigenous Chhau forms, the villagers, especially womenfolk, dance to typical folk songs in groups during any celebration. They have a typical style of draping a sari, and tribal jewellery bedecks them from head to toe during celebratory events.

Every tiny hamlet has a Jaher, which does not have a boundary or any idol to worship. It is a huge open space filled with trees, large and small, with a small demarcation at the centre. It is basically nature that the tribals offer prayers to. They believe that forests are their god, as it is through the forests that they sustain themselves. They consume from the forests and ensure that they protect them. They treat nature as the creator and destroyer. In nature, they find the solution to all their problems and sufferings. Nature is the only force that can make or break their lives.

Those wishing to pray in a Jaher can just walk in, sit peacefully and pray. It is believed that silent prayers are the Santal way of connecting spiritually with nature. There are no rules and no benediction pronounced. People are free to come and go out of the Jaher for communion with god at any point in time.

The common factor binding the whole community is the ability to accept whatever comes its way without any regrets and complaints. Populated with around 4,000–5,000 people, Uparbeda has proudly sent at least fifty of its youths to the defence and paramilitary forces to serve the country. As is their wont, tribals are neither aspirational nor do they hanker for more. All they are concerned about is their identity and belongingness to *jal, jungle aur jameen*.

BIRTH AND EDUCATION

On 20 June 1958, in the Santal-dominated Uparbeda, Putti, more popularly known today as Droupadi Murmu, was born to Singo and Biranchi Narayan Tudu. The Santals celebrate the birth of a girl with much fervour, and Droupadi's birth was a reason for celebration at home.

The name 'Droupadi' was given to her by one of the teachers in school who used to come from another district. Since there were not many teachers in the remote districts, teachers mostly from Cuttack and Bhubaneswar were appointed to remote schools. For these teachers, the tribal name 'Putti' did not mean anything. The Santal tradition states that names do not die in the tribe. So, often, a girl born in the family carries the paternal grandmother's name while boys are named after their paternal grandfather. The teacher, probably unaware of this tradition, changed Putti's name to Droupadi.

Murmu's father, Biranchi Narayan Tudu, was a farmer and a village chieftain, also known as 'sardar' and 'pradhan' in the local language. Her grandfather, too, had been a traditional head, a designated sarpanch of the Gram Panchayat. The pradhans were solely responsible for all the important decisions concerning individuals, community and village. In case of any clash, conflict or decision regarding matrimony or territorial concerns, it was the pradhan whose decision was final. This leadership trait in Tudu seems to have manifested in Murmu, making her an able administrator through her career. Pradhans, since the British rule, have been associated with opulence and affluence. Tudu was also one of the pradhans who were well-to-do until he suffered the wrath of two years of drought (1961–62 and 1964–65). The family was almost in ruins and their finances collapsed.

Pradhans were usually assigned tasks like revenue collection, tax collection and aggregation of agricultural produce from villagers to deposit in the treasury. Even though this practice was discontinued after Independence, pradhans continued to hold power. Even today, some places have pradhans as decision-makers, irrespective of the presence of sarpanches, who are elected as per government rules and regulations.

Murmu began her education in Uparbeda Government Upper Primary School from Classes 1 to 5. Since she was inclined towards education, her father enrolled her in the school after her *khadi chhuan* (the day when a child holds a piece of chalk and writes for the first time). She started attending classes every single day without fail.

In the 1960s, when the education of girls was not considered important, Tudu wanted Murmu to be educated. Emulating her, many other girls were also enrolled into the school by their parents. Those were the days when girls used to be keener about learning household chores than spending the whole day in school studying.

Murmu's friends and teachers remember her as one of the very few who were disciplined and devoted. Time was sacrosanct for her, and she never failed to reach the school first; she was, in fact, the last one to leave as well.

This did not mean that she wasn't involved in household chores. Like her father, her grandmother, who was from Chakradharpur, supported her in her pursuit of higher education. However, it could not be at the cost of her chores. Whenever Murmu wanted to study at home, she used the kerosene lamp for it. But her grandmother ensured the lamp was turned off because she did not want to waste kerosene for studies. 'You are going to school to study, put off that lamp. You must only do household work at home and keep studies for school time,' is what she used to tell Murmu.[3] Therefore, Murmu cleaned the house and utensils and also swept the floors when she was at home.

But Murmu always looked up to her grandmother as an inspiration. She was a multifaceted personality who would be there with the villagers when they needed a doctor to attend to flu cases or child delivery. She was also the one to solve village disputes whenever required. She was the most sought-after person in the village for being relatively educated when others had never gone to school. With her exposure and knowledge, she was the 'agony aunt' who helped sort family fights. She also helped women resolve their health issues and was especially involved in childbirth.

Murmu's school, which was then the only primary school (established in 1901), has now been upgraded to a higher secondary school with classes up to eighth standard. Back then, it had five rooms earmarked for five classes. All the rooms had concrete walls with asbestos roofing, though the floors were cracked and broken. The five classrooms were called Baitarani, Similipal, Bapuji,

---

[3]'Governor Ganeshi Lal, Dharmendra Pradhan and President Murmu Visit Tapoban High School,' YouTube, https://bit.ly/3yXJEPu. Accesed on 21 March 2023.

Nehru and Khadakhai. The student strength of the school when Murmu used to study there stood between fifty and sixty, as there were dropouts every year. The school was co-educational, with a residential facility for the boys, while the girls commuted from their homes. Villagers said that the land allotted to the school had been donated by Murmu's family when times had been good. The headmaster, Basanta Kumar Giri, who used to cycle from Dublabeda, was Murmu's teacher in those five years of primary schooling at Uparbeda.

'Droupadi was self-made. The way she conducted herself in the classroom was an example for other students. It is difficult to remember how good she was at securing marks, but her grasping capacity was exceptional and she was an all-rounder. She was a sprinter and excelled in extracurricular activities like music, dance crafts and arts,' said Giri, a septuagenarian who, along with his wife, spoke unendingly about his beloved student.[4] Murmu's leadership qualities were reflected in her early days in school when she became the class monitor.

The Giri couple was visibly moved while speaking about Murmu's achievement. 'She has become the first citizen of the country,' Giri said, crying. Wiping his tears, he went on to say, '*Tulasi dui patrarubaase* [even two leaves of tulsi spread their fragrance from a distance].... There was something in Droupadi that made her different and unique. We could sense she will do well in life.' Always agile and ready to take instructions from teachers, Murmu was the first to take responsibility and fulfil it—be it cleaning the classroom and blackboard or arranging notebooks.

---

[4] All quotes by Basanta Kumar Giri are from an interview conducted by the author on 13 November 2022.

'Her respect for teachers remains unparalleled even today. We have never seen a student like her who would carry forward every word uttered by teachers as law,' reminisced Giri. He was invited by Murmu to be felicitated during her gubernatorial tenure in Jharkhand. 'What a tribute to a teacher from a student. My heart swelled with pride when I saw her in the Raj Bhavan. I also want to meet her in the Rashtrapati Bhavan, but I don't know when that dream of mine will be fulfilled,' he said with a lot of hope in his eyes. 'She was a blessed child,' said Giri.

Murmu's family was in financial crisis, but that would never reflect on her face. Every day, she would go to school with a smile. Even when she did not have books or other requisites, she would try to get books from friends and study before going home, remembered Giri. 'She was hurriedly noting down something in her notebook late in the evening one day, and I asked her why hasn't she gone home and was still studying at school. She smiled and said, "I am just leaving in a minute." But she did not let me know the reason. I got to know from other students that because she could not take someone else's book home, she would complete the work at school and then leave for home,' said Giri.

After completing primary education up to Class 5, Murmu enrolled into the Middle English (ME) School, Uparbeda, to continue her education for Classes 6 and 7. Her teachers in the ME School, Bisweswar Mohanta and Basudev Behera, also echoed similar sentiments. Behera was inducted into the ME School as a teacher in 1969, soon after his intermediate in arts (IA) examinations.[5] Back

---

[5]Intermediate in arts is the equivalent of modern-day 'plus two', that is, Classes 11 and 12.

then, teachers in schools used to teach all subjects. Since the school did not have government patronage then, it was being managed independently by the village committee. The school had sixty-eight students in Class 6 and sixty-one in Class 7.

'I had the opportunity to teach Droupadi for two months only in Class 6 but I took all her subjects in Class 7,' narrates Behera.[6] 'Murmu's merits as a student cannot be expressed in words,' the teacher said, adding that he cannot explain how exceptional she was. Behra also stated that she was good in academics and ancillary subjects, including dance and music. Her father did not have the capacity to buy her schoolbooks. All her schoolbooks were given to her by seniors. He recalls that she did not have a geometry box. 'I remember giving her one from the school stock. But when she passed Class 7, she came to the school to donate some of her own books, return the ones borrowed and also the geometry box. She said her work with the box is over, but there may be others who would need the books and geometry box,' said Behera, adding that as a child eleven or twelve years old, Murmu was far more understanding than her peers.

Her teachers had many stories of her kindness, daring and diligence to narrate. They stated how, one day, the path to the school was flooded in the absence of fair-weather roads. The water flowed downstream from the mountain ranges, through the Budharana forests nearby and gushed into the village, throwing life out of gear. 'But we suddenly saw Droupadi braving the downpour and reaching the

---

[6]All quotes by Basudev Behera are from an interview conducted by the author on 13 November 2022.

school. We were surprised and asked her how she managed to reach the school and she said that she swam all the way from her home, crossing the overflowing nullah. Such was her passion for studies that no force could deter her from attending classes,' Behera added. She was a skilled swimmer and tree climber and equally good at managing household chores.

Murmu was the one who used to sweep and mop the classroom floor and spread cow dung on it to make it flat and functional, as most portions were chipped. She would prepare dusters at home with torn clothes and take them to the school. 'Droupadi was far ahead of children her age. The peon of the school was fondly addressed as *kaka* by Droupadi and she would take the broom from his hands to sweep the classroom,' Behera said.

'She was not poor, her father was a pradhan, but two droughts in consecutive years had pushed the family to penury,' Behera said, reminiscing about her khadi chhuan on 27 January 1963. '*Mu garbita, bakya nahi kichi kahibaku* [I am proud and running short of words]' was how the teacher explained his feelings on seeing his favourite student as the president of the country.

Her schoolmates said that when teachers used to ask all of them what they aim to become in life, some said doctor and engineer while others wanted to become teachers and farmers. But Murmu was always silent. She would smile and giggle. 'Her silence has proven her strength more than words. She was focussed only on studying well, leaving the rest to destiny. Now what she has achieved is beyond the reach of anyone. We are lucky to have had her as a student,' Behera adds.

Murmu only had one frock to wear to school. So, every

day after returning from school, she would clean it and keep it with care for the next day. However, she was never concerned about not having more clothes. She was happy with whatever she had, reflecting the temperament of her tribe, which was evolved enough not to regret or complain.

CLASS MONITOR TO 'COUNTRY MONITOR'

A true friend to all her classmates, Murmu was very close to Tapati Mandal.[7] Both Murmu and Mandal studied together till Class 7, after which Mandal got married while Murmu left for Bhubaneswar for higher studies.

Mandal still remembers Murmu's recital of her favourite Odia poem:

Sundara jetiki, andhara setiki,
Ehi je gahanabana,
Tenu tu sankalpa patha re atala,
Achala raha re mana.
Aagare padichi patha bahu dura,
Chaliba paain bi baaki,
Chalibi chalibi napadibi thaki,
Mudiba agaru aakhi.

[As beautiful and dark
Are the dense forests,
Be resolute to walk the path of duty,
With an unwavering mind.
There are miles to go
And distance to walk,

---

[7] All quotes by Tapati Mandal are from an interview conducted by the author on 13 November 2022

I will walk and keep walking
Until I close my eyes.]⁸

Terming her as a friend, philosopher and guide, Tapati says she missed Murmu ever since they parted ways. It was only during summer and winter vacations when Murmu returned to the village that the two friends used to catch up. 'We would spend time with each other at her house or ours. But after marriage, I had to shift to other places and lost touch with her,' reminisced Tapati.

However, Tapati, who has returned to her native village after decades, has kept abreast of all the news about Murmu from her family in Uparbeda. She said:

> I tried to keep track of her even though I was away. I was happy to know that she has become the councillor for Rairangpur. When she fought elections, I could not believe it. But I got used to her achievements with time. She became a minister and also Jharkhand's governor, and when I got to know about her becoming president, I was very happy, not only because she is my friend but because her struggles and journey would inspire many other girls to choose a good way of life.

She, however, was excited to narrate their meetups when Murmu visited the village for some public functions. They would miss no opportunity to catch up.

Janani janamamaati, ehi mora gaan, bhuli nahi na
bhulibi kebetaara naa.
Ta chhatire paada dei, sikhili mu chaali, khelikheli udaibi
kete dhuli baali....

---

⁸Author's translation

[The motherland is revered as the mother, I would never forget her, I learnt to walk here, I learnt to play here.]⁹

As Murmu crooned these verses, Tapati used to tease her by saying, let us see how much you remember and take care of your motherland. But now everyone knows how she has made the name of her village in the true sense. Murmu has often mentioned the importance of the motherland and mother tongue in most of her deliberations, not only during her presidential tenure but even during her term as the governor.

The importance of the motherland that Murmu had expressed in her childhood lived on in her adulthood and expressed itself through action. Even today, when she addresses meetings, motherland and mother tongue are recurrent themes. She brought about a lot of changes to her village after getting a seat in the ministry in Naveen Patnaik's BJD–BJP alliance government. Between 2000 and 2004, when she was the commerce and transport minister, Uparbeda villagers got pucca roads as well as the bridge to connect the village to Kaduani Chhak. Even electricity connection, water supply and other development works were done during that phase. However, only one area in the village, Munda Sahi, was left—it got electricity soon after she became the president.

Since their parents were family friends, Tapati and Murmu spent many days in each other's company. Tapati shared that Murmu's most loved subject was literature and she would recite many poems and sections from memory in various programmes in the school. 'Recently, when I

---

⁹Author's translation

met her just before her presidential nominations, she was the same as she had been in the school days. Nothing has changed about her over the years. She continues to be as warm, child-like, caring and soft-spoken and duty-bound as she was earlier. I never found her to be haughty, and she has made us proud with her achievements,' said Tapati, adding that Murmu was consistently the class monitor for her leadership qualities. 'Now she is the country monitor,' Mandal added with a sense of pride.

Ramachandra Murmu, her classmate in Government Upper Primary School in Uparbeda, recalled that he and Murmu would often share food from the same container on the school campus. Settled as a farmer in Uparbeda, Ramachandra said that everyone in the president's hometown is proud of her achievements. 'But I am not sure if I should use *tu* (informal address) or *aap* (address with respect) when we talk next,' he added.[10]

When Murmu went to Bhubaneswar for higher education, Ramachandra left for Raipur. But he confesses to having studied till graduation with the hope that he would get into politics. And when he returned to Rairangpur, he got into political activities in the district. It was only when his childhood friend, Murmu, contested the elections that there was no stopping Ramachandra. He took responsibility of looking after all the vehicles that were put to use during campaigning and also handled electioneering in some pockets. He said that he still is a friend, proud of another friend's success. 'Just that there will henceforth be a protocol in meeting and talking to her,' he stated.

---

[10]'Not Sure If We Could Still Address Murmu Informally, Say Friends Back Home,' *Deccan Herald*, 24 July 2022, http://bit.ly/3ZZL07G. Accessed on 13 March 2023.

THE SHOCK OF CITY LIFE

After completing Class 7, Murmu was firm about continuing higher education, and that was possible only in Bhubaneswar. Uparbeda had no school for higher classes and those who wanted to continue had to go out of the village.

On her father's advice, she decided to meet Kartik Majhi, her relative and the then Swatantra Party MLA from Rairangpur, who was scheduled to attend a political meeting in Rairangpur. Fearlessly, she gathered her academic certificates and left to meet Majhi with a request to help her enrol in Government Girls High School in Bhubaneswar. As the public meeting was underway, she waited for a while and, as soon as the programme ended, mustered up the courage to go up to the dais and show her certificates to the MLA. She requested him to help her get admission in a higher education school. Majhi, impressed with her courage, conviction and credentials on the marksheet, asked his staff to collect her documents and arrange for her admission in a residential school in Bhubaneswar.

In a few days, Murmu was called for admission to the Government Girls High School, Unit 2, in the state capital. With the dream of studying and doing something in life, she left Uparbeda. She was unconcerned about everything other than studies but could not hide her apprehensions about a new life, as she was preparing to go to a new place with no one to call her own. With one or two frocks and a little money in hand, she stepped out with her father with dreams in her eyes and hope in her heart.

As it is, the roads from the district to the capital were bad back then. Even now, there is no train connectivity to places beyond Baripada in the district, and the demand for the same has been gaining momentum for years. There were no roads laid, nor was there a means of transport to reach the place from where people could board a bus. In the case of women, it was even more problematic, as there was no bridge on the river Kanu; this was a barrier between the villages on one side and the state highway at Kaduani Chhak. Braving all odds, the father–daughter duo reached there. Since in those days, only one or two government buses plied that route, they had to wait for hours before boarding one.

A sense of uncertainty was looming large in Murmu's mind, which she has talked about on various occasions, but she was undeterred.[11] After hours of travelling, the father–daughter duo reached the capital city, which was very different from the place Murmu had grown up in. The fast-paced city was a shock for her, the life and times were different, the lifestyle was more complicated and food habits were the opposite of what they used to be back home. But she was not one to look back. She reached the campus close to the bus terminal and got admission in the school. She also got accommodation in a hostel on the same campus that was meant for outstation Adivasi students. Every dormitory in the hostel had seven to eight beds and a little space to store belongings. The hostel was later named Kuntala Kumari Sabat Hostel and continues to house SC/ST students till date.

In a world that seemed alien, Murmu wanted to be one of the many faces in the crowd. She wanted to belong to

---

[11]'Dr Itirani Samanta in Conversation with Droupadi Murmu' (Video in Odia), YouTube, http://bit.ly/3Jrdhib. Accessed on 9 March 2023.

the place. The momentary feeling of being out of place was unnerving, but she was strong in her conviction and willpower. As her father wanted to return to the village the next day, she was a little worried by the thought that she was going to be a lone fighter.[12] Since all the girls who stayed in the hostel and studied in the school were from far off places, they did not form friendships quickly. She prepared herself, a child who was hardly twelve or thirteen years old, to bid adieu to her father. That day ushered in a completely new life for Murmu.

Inhibited in a place away from her hometown, she, like her roommates, started going to school the next day onwards. By nature, she was not very talkative or loud, and adjusting to the new environment was not easy for her. There were many girls from tribal backgrounds, and one of them, named Dangi Murmu, clicked with her soon. But even then, Murmu preferred to speak less and observe more, while Dangi was just the opposite.

Soon, Murmu made a few friends in the class and hostel. The regimen in the hostel was so strict that everything had to be done in a disciplined way. There was a fixed time for every activity, be it eating, bathing, studying or sleeping. Everyone followed it. The hostel superintendent, Shantilata Gochchayat, was known to be a strict disciplinarian, and no rules could be bent for anyone. Gochchayat is no more, but she spoke to Murmu a few days before her death. However, her daughters, Chinmayee (Chunni) and Tanmayee, who happen to be good friends of Murmu, are in touch with their friend, Madam President.

---

[12]Ibid.

Murmu's friends described her as an introvert who would choose her words before speaking. She was receptive and attentive in the classroom, sat towards the last benches and was diligent to a fault. She was one of the very few students participating in various debates and elocution competitions. She also used to participate in sports and secure medals. With a strong physique, Murmu got into the National Cadet Corps (NCC), which girls her age were never keen on joining. She regularly attended NCC sessions and was a part of the Republic Day and Independence Day parades. Even then, her enthusiasm for anything patriotic was palpable. She was also chosen as the best cadet in the school.

As per her classmates, she never used to go out of the campus or even had a desire to do so. Financially, the family was in such a situation that Murmu's father, while dropping her to Bhubaneswar, had not been able to give her any money to spend. But since the government was taking care of her tuition fees and accommodation, including food, she never opened up about the need for money.

Every need of the SC/ST students was taken care of, but they were not allowed to step out of the campus unless the matron accompanied them. The girls were allowed to go out in groups and the matron or any other staff of the school would accompany them if there was any need to buy anything. This was not only true for the students of the high school but even for college-going students who continued to live in the same hostel as not many colleges had hostel accommodation then.

Gochchayat, a Gandhian, had been sent from an NGO called Utkal Nabajiban Mandal, also known as Nabakrushna Choudhury Ashram, in Angul to take care of the students. She had enough experience working with the likes of freedom fighters Rama Devi Choudhury, Malati Choudhury (Numa) and Nabakrushna Choudhury, who later had a brief stint as the CM of Odisha. The three people were instrumental in setting up the ashram, which helped Adivasi children from remote parts of the state pursue an education. While Numa used to work for the poor and downtrodden and also fought in the war of Independence shoulder-to-shoulder with her husband, Nabakrushna, her sister-in-law, Rama Devi, had taken it upon herself to run an Adivasi boarding school at Angul. The school is now known as Bajirout Chhatrabas, named after the youngest freedom fighter from Odisha. It was here that Gochchayat was working with Numa when the government wanted her to join the Adivasi hostel in the Unit 2 high school. She came to Bhubaneswar with her daughters to join the school. Her experience of working with SC/ST students, particularly girls, was the reason she was chosen to handle the work, and she performed her duties to the best of her abilities.

Murmu seemed to be in awe of Gochchayat and considered her an ideal. Before passing away, she had reflected on some memories pertaining to Murmu and her daughters, who were classmates. The twin daughters of Gochchayat used to spend a lot of time at the hostel, waiting for their mother to finish her school work. Thus, both got some time to spend with their classmates in the hostel after classes.

Remembering her days in the school, Chinmayee said, 'Murmu was always seen subdued, which was natural for most girls coming from a very backward place. She kept to herself and was very often seen busy in her own work, be it study or cleaning or completing homework. She was good in sports, games and also music.'[13]

Gochchayat had frequent interactions with each hostel boarder. She used to take sessions with hostel girls separately, just as we have motivational classes nowadays. Students who were feeling a little low or sad would be tutored by Gochchayat. So, directly and indirectly, Chinmayee and Tanmayee knew Murmu closely, as their mother shared stories of the girls who often had struggles in life.

'It was those times when school life meant classes and some fun with friends, but Murmu was quiet and kept to herself. She was studious, disciplined and attentive,' said Chinmayee. She also acknowledged that whatever Murmu has achieved is by sheer hard work, grit and determination along with the zeal to serve the society.

She remembers that every letter a boarder wrote had to be approved by her mother.

> In those days, the boarders used to go out of the hostel to their native places only during summer vacations. So as per hostel regulations, postcards were the only medium the students could use to communicate with their parents. Additionally, my mother, as the superintendent, was rule-bound to go through all the boarders' postcards before they were dispatched. Once, she found that Murmu had written to her father to send her ten rupees. On reading the postcard, she had wanted Murmu to change the content, lest it hurt her father. My mother made her understand that her basic requirements were being looked after by the

---

[13] All quotes by Chinmayee Gochchayat are from an interview conducted by the author on 28 November 2022.

government and that she would not need that amount at all. Having understood it, she changed the content of the postcard. This is why Murmu remains indebted to my mother. Before my mother passed away a few years ago, Murmu had spoken with her and expressed her gratitude for guiding her. Though she had promised to meet my mother soon, official work kept her tied up and my mother passed away meanwhile.

Dangi, who stayed in the same dormitory at the girls' hostel, has since then remained a constant friend of Murmu. They spent lot of time together. She attended the swearing-in ceremony at Rashtrapati Bhavan and vouched for the all-rounder Murmu during her school days. 'She was an expert in stitching Sal leaf plates that tribals traditionally learn in the family. Besides, she used to knit beautiful dusters with torn clothes,' remembered Dangi, who also shared the hostel room with Murmu in school. 'I can bet no school even now has the discipline that was the way of life during our school days. Anyone and everyone who had been under the supervision of Shantilata Gochchayat in the school is well settled and established. It is the rigours of time-bound discipline that made us what we are today,' said Dangi, who retired from the Central Board of Excise and Customs in April 2018.

AN EDUCATION WITH TWO FROCKS

Murmu remained a student of the Government Girls High School till Class 11, as was the rule of the Board of Secondary Education, and then joined the Rama Devi Women's College, Bhubaneswar. Chinmayee and Tanmayee also studied for their IA and BA with Murmu in the same college. While Chinmayee had difficulties remembering smaller details, she clearly recalled that Murmu was a good orator and had the gift of the gab but rarely showed it. 'It was during competitions that we heard her speaking very articulately, and when I hear her now as the president, I can recollect how good a speaker she was and how she has honed her skills,' she reminisced.

Also a Santal, Dangi remembered the common factors between her and Murmu that have kept them bound as friends even in the present day. Their food habits, lifestyle, language and roots in the Mayurbhanj district kept them together in school days. She fondly remembered how they used to compete over everything, like kids usually do. Be it eating, completing their studies or sleeping, the two friends would start a competition that would end with a clear winner. 'Let's see who finishes first, who wakes up first, who comes to eat first and there were many such things. We never had any hobbies or keenness like girls of the present day. Our viewpoint was narrow as we stayed bound within the boundaries of the school and hostel. So we did these small things like competing with each other in such trivial issues and that is how our time was spent,' said Dangi.

A black-and-white group photo of Murmu, Dangi and Sumitra Kisku, another friend and classmate of Murmu in school and roommate in the hostel, in Class 8 is found in the same dormitory of the hostel even today. Dangi said that they wore each other's frocks if the other had washed hers. 'None of us had plenty. She had her share of struggles and I had mine, but we never made them issues to bother with. Both of us had two to three dresses to wear in school and hostel,' she remembered. The government used to provide a stipend amount for the girls and the frocks would be made with ₹2 per metre cloth.[14]

Dangi also mentioned that in the school hostel, there were 'time ministers' and 'food ministers' for hostel management. While the food minister would ensure food was prepared well and served, the time minister used to ring the bell when it was time to wake up or leave for school. 'Shantilata didi used to ask us to keep the windows open during study hours so that she could sit in her room and still keep a watch on us to see if we were studying or not. That is the reason each one of us scored well, though we did not know what use these subjects would be in later life,' she recollected. 'Since most did not know the importance of subjects, despite being good at math, the girls would opt for home science, either because that would help us learn things that could be put to use in family life or because we would not be pressurized to study hard for as difficult a subject as math.'

Dangi, however, rued that they could not access many facilities for students in general and adivasi students in particular. 'We were happy with the food supplied to us and never wished for anything. But we never had the resources or the privilege to even enjoy with our peer group. We had two school uniforms. The one we wore today would be cleaned at night and dried while the second one would be worn the next day,' she revealed.

Dangi also came from a family that was financially weak. She remembered that because she did not have the paltry sum of ₹60, she had to miss attending the NCC

---

[14]"Dr Itirani Samanta in Conversation with Droupadi Murmu' (Video in Odia), YouTube, http://bit.ly/3Jrdhib. Accessed on 9 March 2022.

event in New Delhi. 'Our parents did not have that much money to spare for going to Delhi. So I backed out,' she reminisced. Murmu was as good in the NCC as she was in her studies and sports. 'She was an all-rounder. She always participated in all such extracurricular events. Even now, she sings so well. We heard her when she was the governor and we, a group of friends, went to visit her at the Raj Bhavan of Jharkhand. Her voice is the same as it was years ago. The tribal dances and music are her forte,' Dangi added.

After Class 11, Dangi left for Baripada to study IA and BA while Murmu stayed back in Bhubaneswar. In these five years, the two friends lost touch with each other. However, after graduating, when Murmu joined the irrigation department of the Odisha government, Dangi started working with the central excise department. Since both of them lived in Bhubaneswar, they got in touch, and from then on, they have remained connected till now. 'Back then, there was no cell phone or normal telephone to be in touch, but we used to visit each other at the rented rooms we stayed in while working,' said Dangi.

Murmu's college mate, Suchitra Samal, said that she is the same person that she was when they met for the first time. 'I was pleasantly surprised when she called me recently. I wasn't expecting a call from her amid her busy schedule. I had wished her earlier on her success when she became the governor and now as she was elected president,' Samal said.[15]

---

[15] 'Not Sure if We Could Still Address Murmu Informally, Say Friends Back Home,' *Deccan Herald*, 24 July 2022, http://bit.ly/3ZZL07G. Accessed on 13 March 2023.

A FERTILE SOIL: UPARBEDA

Apart from being the birthplace of President Murmu, Uparbeda has the unique distinction of having sent four of its residents to the Odisha Assembly. Coincidentally, all four have their houses located one after the other in the village—Salkhan Murmu's house is followed by Droupadi Murmu's, then Kartik Majhi's and finally comes Bhabendra Nath Majhi's.

The politically active village saw the birth of a successful politician in Kartik Majhi, who became the first person to win the Rairangpur (ST) seat in 1967 as a Swatantra Party candidate. He also became the first from the constituency to get a seat in the ministry, taking the reins of the finance department when R.N. Singh Deo was the CM of Odisha between 1967 and 1971. He was also given the home, urban development works and transport portfolios during the same period.

Bhabendra Nath Majhi, also from the village, contested for the Assembly on a Congress ticket and won. But he passed away on 3 March 1986, a year after being elected.

Salkhan Murmu, founder and national president of Jharkhand Disom Party, also traces his roots to Uparbeda as his father was born and brought up in the village. However, he was born in Karandih, within the police limits of Parasudih in East Singhbhum, Jharkhand, where his father had migrated in search of a job. But his connection to the state remained strong enough, so much so that he contested and won the twelfth and thirteenth Lok Sabha elections (1998–2004) from Mayurbhanj constituency during the Atal Bihari Vajpayee government. A commerce postgraduate, Salkhan Murmu worked in Tata Steel

Jamshedpur for ten years before quitting in 1989 to join politics. Salkhan joined the Adivasi Sengel Abhiyan for a separate state of Jharkhand and successfully led many rallies. The BJP and its sitting BJD MLA from Morada (in Mayurbhanj district), Rajkishore Das, had reportedly approached him to join the saffron party with an assurance that he would be given a ticket to contest the 1996 Lok Sabha election. He did contest as a BJP candidate but lost.[16] Murmu got elected from Rairangpur to the twelfth (2000–04) and thirteenth (2004–09) Assemblies.

Elected twice to the Lok Sabha with a BJP ticket from the Mayurbhanj seat in 1998 and 1999, Salkhan refused to contest the next election, as he wanted to work for tribal self-rule system reforms. He met Murmu at her Rairangpur residence on 18 April 2022 and discussed a wide range of issues pertaining to tribal welfare and self-rule. He also called her again on 22 June to wish her after her nomination as a presidential candidate was made public.

Though Uparbeda is now dotted with concrete houses, most people have retained their previous dwelling units as marks of the past. Every house has kept intact the hutments made of mud and clay as well as thatched roofing.

Murmu's house, too, has been concretized, but a portion of the house still has the old tenement towards the back. These tiny, dingy rooms that are cleaner than tiled homes mutely witnessed the evolution of a country's president. Painted in yellow, a colour considered auspicious, the concrete house is now being used by Murmu's nephew and his family of six. There are washrooms in and water supply to

---

[16] 'Mayurbhanj Lok Sabha Election Result,' *Result University*, https://bit.ly/40D2xD3. Accessed on 27 March 2023.

most houses, which were hard to imagine six decades earlier when Murmu was growing up. According to her relatives, electricity also remains constant in the village.

In the portion of the house where Murmu grew up, nothing has changed. The rooms remain the same as a mark of Madam President's past. A small *dibiri* (a kerosene lantern) is still hanging on one of the walls, and the kitchen is still as it was years ago. The rooms stand testimony to the struggles of the family and remind everyone that people from the lowest echelons of the society can also reach the pinnacle of success with struggle and hard work.

'She loves to spend time with us here, but it has been long since she has stepped here, not even after her nomination in the presidential elections,' said Dulari Tudu. She went on to explain Murmu's simple way of life by showing the rooms she spent her childhood in. 'Pakhala and saag are her all-time favourites, and she has stopped consuming even onion and garlic for quite some time now,' explained Dulari.

In the backyard of the house in the village, a massive telecom tower has been recently set up. A lot of vacant space is also lying unutilized, which has all types of fruit-bearing plants and a good number of chicks loitering around. Not one person was seen out of their homes on the forenoon in November 2022 in the area that has nurtured four former MLAs and gained them prominence in politics.

Surprisingly, though, Dulari, along with her family, still goes shopping to Rairangpur on two-wheelers. The President's family members have no airs and maintain the same lifestyle as earlier. This is perhaps a reflection of Murmu's personality. She has contined to be humble even after becoming the first citizen of the country.

Without realizing what was in store, Murmu stepped into the precincts of her college. Her aim was clear but path uncharted. Taking one step at a time, she embraced a new life, a different world altogether than the one she had lived in until then. College days and a job immediately after changed the course of life and how!

2

An Emancipation of Sorts: College and First Job

After completing her school education at the Government Girls High School, Unit 2, in 1974, Murmu enrolled in Rama Devi Women's College in Bhubaneswar for a two-year IA course, becoming the first girl from her village to have stepped into a college.

Rama Devi Women's College was (and still is) one of the premiere institutes of higher education in Odisha. Those enrolling into it are considered privileged and fortunate for being associated with the legacy of Rama Devi Choudhury, one of the leading women freedom fighters of the Indian struggle for independence. As a humble tribute to the values and sacrifices she stood for, Rama Devi was adoringly called 'Maa'. She was also a social reformer who brought about revolution in matters of caste and untouchability.

As the president, Murmu has often mentioned her during her deliberations as one of the many personalities who have inspired her immensely, and the reason is understandable.[1]

---

[1] 'Odisha Should Lead India's Growth Story: President Murmu,' *The New Indian Express*, 11 November 2022, https://bit.ly/3YlQ70K. Accessed on 3 March 2023.

FOOTPRINTS IN THE SANDS OF TIME

Rama Devi was the daughter of Gopal Ballav Das and the niece of Utkal Gaurab Madhusudan Das. At the tender age of fifteen, she married Gopabandhu Choudhury, then a deputy collector who later became a freedom fighter.

On 23 March 1921, Rama Devi met Mahatma Gandhi and Kasturba Gandhi at Binod Behari in Cuttack, where they were addressing a rally, and decided to dedicate herself to the country's cause. With son Manamohan and daughter Annapurna, she followed in her husband's footsteps to join the Non-Cooperation Movement. She organized activities like spinning khadi and participated in Gandhi's call for the prohibition of liquor. She also spoke out against untouchability. She was arrested and imprisoned in 1930 for leading the Salt Satyagraha at Srijanga in Balasore district and Kujang in Jagatsinghpur district. After her release, she was arrested again two years later while taking the solemn oath on 26 January 1932 for *purnaswaraj*, or complete independence, of the country.

After she was released, Rama Devi founded an ashram called Seva Ghar (now Gopabandhu Choudhury College) at Ramachandrapur in Jajpur district with the purpose of helping rebuild the flood-ravaged villages along the Brahmani. Gandhi reached the ashram and inaugurated it on 20 May 1934 in the midst of the Harijan Padayatra in Odisha. However, on 9 August 1942, Rama Devi was arrested again. It was the day Gandhi called for the Quit India Movement.[2] She was in the Cuttack jail with her husband, son, daughter, brother-in-law Nabakrushna, sister-

---

[2]'About Rama Devi,' *Rama Devi Women's University*, https://bit.ly/3IMhlb7. Accessed on 3 March 2023.

in-law Malati Devi and son-in-law Sarat Chandra. On the eve of Independence, Rama Devi was nominated as the state convener of the Kasturba National Memorial Trust, and she took the opportunity to launch several programmes for the emancipation and empowerment of women. These made an indelible mark on the mind and heart of Murmu.

Even after Independence, Rama Devi worked for the Bhoodan and Gramdan movements of Acharya Vinoba Bhave. With her husband, she walked 4,000 km across the state to propagate the message of gifting land and wealth to the landless and poor.

Murmu has often cited the selfless dedication of Rama Devi that drove her to try and better the lives of women and the poor.

The erstwhile Government Women's College established in 1964 and affiliated to Utkal University was rechristened as Rama Devi Women's College, Bhubaneswar, when it was shifted to its current 28 acre campus near Rupali Square, Bhubaneswar, on 1 January 1969. This is where Murmu felt the winds of change and laid the foundation of her future journey.

NOT A PENNY WASTED: COLLEGE AND ACTIVISM

When Murmu got into college with a few of her school friends, she met other girls like her who had stepped into Bhubaneswar for the first time and came from various parts of the state. Murmu could identify with their reserved and shy nature. She tried to make them feel comfortable as someone who had been in the capital for four years already, and that is where she started guiding the new entrants. Since there was no hostel for SC/ST women college-goers, Murmu and many of her ilk from far-off places continued to stay at the same Unit 2 school hostel meant for Adivasis. It was only after a couple of years that the college hostel for SC/ST students was constructed. Similarly, a hostel for the general students was also inaugurated on the campus soon after.

Those close to Murmu said that maybe she was apprehensive about doing anything and being critiqued, and this was why she kept to herself and was not keen to mingle unless needed. The reason was probably that, unlike others, her problems were plenty and her aim behind being educated was different from that of other girls. For her, graduating would mean that she would have the ability to take up a job and earn for the family. Thus, she would remain glued to textbooks, focussing on her studies and refusing to be distracted by anything.

As the college was situated near Rupali Square on Janpath, one of the busiest roads in the capital city of Bhubaneswar, the students could see the fast-paced traffic on the street from inside the classrooms. Murmu would often stand at the portico and observe her classmates and the outside world.[3]

Recently, while addressing students of the varsity during the convocation ceremony, the president took a trip down memory lane, stating that she still remembers the aroma of food floating in from the college canteen. 'But I used to divert my attention towards other things. I used to stare at the *thela wala* (the person who sells things on a cart) who was serving lemon slices with salt, but my financial condition did not permit me to buy that. If I could lay my

---

[3] "President Droupadi Murmu Graces the Second Convocation of Rama Devi Women's University, Bhubaneswar' (Video in Odia), YouTube, http://bit.ly/3F6l6Hm. Accessed on 9 March 2023

hands on 25 paise worth groundnuts, it was too good for me.'[4] She also spoke about how the college had girls from all sections of society, and she was one of the many from marginalized communities. Like in school, it took her some time to mingle with her classmates.[5]

In one of her interviews, Murmu reminisced:

> Even though I was the only one from the village to study IA and BA, most of us were bottled up. Belonging to a very conservative village and suddenly getting exposed to the city life could not have possibly changed our outlook so soon. We had not much knowledge of the world at large. Moreover, rules were so stringent that whenever we went out with friends to buy some essentials, there were always one or two attendants with us. They would accompany us from the hostel and leave us back there. Walking on the roads meant looking straight, not to the right or left.[6]

There was no dress code for college students, and Murmu, along with her friends, used to wear saris to college.

As she did not talk much, either in hostel or college, most friends felt that she was introverted. Chinmayee, her friend from school, said:

> We used to have fun in the classroom when there were no teachers but she would be engrossed in some book or keep writing something in her notebook. Even when

---

[4]Ibid; author's translation.
[5]Ibid.
[6]'An Exclusive Interview with India's First Tribal President, Draupadi Murmu by Dr. Itirani Samanta,' YouTube, http://bit.ly/420iZ1w. Accessed on 10 March 2023.

we broke for lunch break, she would never be a part of the gathering that ate at the canteen. We felt she was feeling a little conscious about belonging to a completely different community.

The subjects that most IA students, including Murmu, opted for were history, political science, home science, logic and philosophy. 'She was not exceptionally brilliant but certainly studious,' said Chinmayee. 'She would score good marks but her aim was to get into a job as soon as college education gets over.' After college, the twins Chinmayee and Tanmayee lost touch with Murmu. It was only when she became the transport minister that they remembered their classmate Droupadi Tudu becoming Murmu post marriage and getting into politics. Chinmayee stated:

> It was a pleasant shock to us because the way we last saw her in college, we never knew she would become a minister in Odisha government. We all tried to touch base with her and finally got her telephone number. I spoke to her quite a few times but it was only when she became the Jharkhand governor that our ties got strengthened.

'Life in college was different and there were fewer interactions as Murmu was characteristically not as loud or boisterous as the other girls were. We used to go to the college gate and have *gupchup* and chaat but I never saw her doing all that. She was content with just attending classes and going back to hostel,' Chinmayee described Murmu's college days. She added that Murmu was an active participant in plays and performances on the campus.

Knowing that every penny matters, Murmu never spent

on anything other than essentials, like the money required to commute between her village and Bhubaneswar, till she completed her graduation in 1979.

'I used to have a couple of saris even in college and never wanted more. Never did I go for a movie or theatre or engaged in recreational activities as I did not have the means to afford [them] but during BA, things were a little different,' recollected Murmu, much before her presidential nomination.[7] Later, however, she said in an interview that in the eight years she spent in Bhubaneswar, she had watched only one movie, *Gapa Hele Bi Sata,* at Ravi Talkies near Old Town.[8]

The vacation calendar for school and college was more or less similar, and those were the times when Murmu would travel back to her village until the academic session restarted. Buses were the only mode of transport that was accessible and available. Girls from nearby villages in the district would often travel together to ensure that they had company since the journey was arduous. Though Murmu has never spoken openly about the trials and tribulations of a lone Adivasi girl commuting to and from far-off Bhubaneswar, sometimes alone and at times with a few friends, most of her generation agrees that the days of travelling were hard times. The journey involved hours of arduous bus rides. The buses were in a pitiable condition and there was the difficulty of changing buses en route. 'We all faced such hard situations. In fact, we became habituated to such rides as we knew that even if

---

[7]Ibid.
[8]Pradhan, Ashok and Hemanta Pradhan, 'Commitment to Education One Constant in Droupadi Murmu's Career,' *The Times of India,* 22 July 2022, https://bit.ly/3kLmqso. Accessed on 3 March 2023.

we complain, it would not change anything,' said Delha Soren, Murmu's college senior, hostel mate and, later, roommate.[9]

The BJP leader Surama Padhy, who went on to become a minister during the BJD–BJP government in Odisha, was also Murmu's junior during their BA. While Padhy had taken up Sanskrit and home science, Murmu opted for economics and political science. Sharing her anecdotes, she recalled that during their graduation days, the Indira Gandhi Post-Matric Adivasi Women's Hostel had come up on the RD campus. Thus, the girls staying in the high school hostel had shifted there. Padhy remembered Murmu having raised the issue of food at the new hostel.

> She was the hostel mess in-charge. So everyone confided in her about the bad quality of food being provided. Since I was her junior, I would always support her in the causes she took up. Moreover, my friends were also staying in the same hostel. We all decided to take action and went to the college authorities for a discussion, after which the menu was revamped and the quality improved. She was also the one to take the lead in organizing theatre and other cultural events in the college.
>
> No matter how calm Didi was during her IA days, I have seen her raising her voice during the graduation classes. But we gelled well because we both fought for genuine concerns in the college. She gained prominence in the college during graduation days and was as much a participant in cultural events

---

[9]All quotes by Delha Soren are from an interview conducted by the author on 2 January 2023.

as she was involved in students' issues. I remember going together with her to sort out issues with college authorities many times.[10]

Padhy added that it was during those days that both she and Murmu took part in student politics. This seems to have laid the foundation for both these leaders, who went on to fight elections, won and became ministers in the government. And their political journeys continue even today. Padhy is currently active in the state BJP functions and is looked up to as one of the probable winners in the 2024 Assembly Elections.

After graduation, however, she lost touch with Murmu for a few years, since Murmu started working, while Padhy went to another college for her postgraduation. But it was their involvement in people's affairs that brought them together after years. When Murmu contested the Rairangpur Notified Area Council (NAC) elections with the BJP's support, Padhy met her. A few years later, both women contested the elections when the BJD and BJP were coalition partners in Odisha. Padhy fought from Ranpur constituency in Nayagarh, while Murmu contested from Rairangpur. Murmu was the commerce and transport minister in the coalition government from 2000 till 2004, and Padhy was cooperation minister from 2004 till 2009.

THE JOB: SOREN'S STORY

Just as Murmu completed her graduation, she came across a Government of Odisha advertisement about recruitment for around 400–500 junior assistants in various departments,

---

[10] Quote from an interview conducted by the author on 21 January 2023

and the selection was to be done through viva voce only. Even though she wished to continue studying further, life did not give her that liberty, as she had to earn soon to support herself and her family. Without wanting to let the opportunity slip through her hands, Murmu applied for the position and appeared for the test.

Qualifying for the job was the first step in her life towards emancipation. 'It was morally obligatory for me to do something for my family, my parents and brothers. If I failed to lend help to my family even God would not excuse me. This assistant job in the irrigation department in 1979 made me self-sufficient and also let me to help my father run the family,' said Murmu in an interview.[11]

During those days, not many women, particularly in Adivasi communities, worked after basic education. Most tended to go along with the family's decision to get married and settle down, like Murmu's friend Tapati. However, Murmu knew other women who studied and worked too, like Delha Soren, her college senior who used to stay in the same girls' hostel meant for SC/ST students and also belonged to Mayurbhanj district. When both women started working, Soren felt that people did not look at them with respect, especially because they were first-generation working women from Adivasi families. But Murmu was habituated to this and stood strong in her conviction.

Though Soren was not able to recollect if Murmu faced any issues as a working woman during those days, she said that everyone faced these issues and Murmu must have too. The difference was that Murmu's aim was clear

---

[11]'Dr Itirani Samanta in Conversation with Droupadi Murmu' (Video in Odia), YouTube, http://bit.ly/3Jrdhib. Accessed on 9 March 2022; author's translation.

and she cared little for any deterrence. Snide, though subtle, remarks were common, added Soren. During Murmu's term at the irrigation office, she was known as a hard worker. While there were many who encouraged her, some others did not. Soren, who joined the accountant general's (AG's) office in Bhubaneswar, was on the lookout for a house to stay on rent and, at the same time, Murmu thought it made sense to share a house. Soren stated:

> We discussed sharing an accommodation. But in those days, getting a good house on rent was not easy for single working women. Both of us applied to the government for allotment of a house, and that was sanctioned. We got a house in Unit 4, AG Colony, and decided to shift. But the house was allotted to four women, Murmu, me and two other government employees.

While Soren and Murmu shared one room, the two others stayed in the second room. They used to cook their food and leave for office in the same rickshaw—Murmu to the irrigation department and Soren to the AG office. Soren recollects:

> Droupadi had always wanted a modest life. She never aspired for more and did not hanker for money or clothes. She would never discuss her financial hardships she was facing back home with me. We used to live with the basics as far as food was concerned and had two to three saris for office that were like a uniform because none of us felt the need to flaunt anything.

Nothing in life deterred Murmu. With a monthly salary of ₹255, she used to pay the house rent of ₹60, keep some money for her expenses and send the rest to her father back in the village. 'It was difficult to manage with such a small amount for a month, but then there was no other way to deal with it. I wanted to be financially helpful and also become self-sufficient. I was ready to slog on an equal platform as men,' Murmu said.[12] Because of the challenges she faced and the struggles she overcame, she has given a lot of importance to women's education and empowerment. Not only when she was a minister in Odisha but also as governor and now as president, she has often deliberated on the importance of women and their education besides financial independence. She has been vocal about saving girl children much before the campaign was kicked off by PM Modi.

Soren added, 'She was an avid reader. In those days, buying books was not easy but she managed to get them from libraries and would read till late at night.' She and Murmu had many things in common—their backgrounds, upbringing and academics were similar due to their native places in the same district and both of them being Santali. So, their food habits and lifestyle did not have any differences. Soren recalled:

> We had a lot to share between ourselves after office hours. Times were stringent and so were the rules. We went to office together in a three-wheeler rickshaw at 10.00 a.m. and returned walking because that helped us fetch vegetables and other essentials from the Unit 4 market nearby. Moreover, we used to talk about a lot of issues while coming back. If that was also not enough, we would talk for hours while cooking, sometimes late in the evening as well.

---

[12]Ibid.

However, they never discussed their personal problems. Soren knew Murmu had a lot of liabilities to take care of and her salary was not enough to give her a free hand. 'I did not send money to my home as there was no requirement. I had lost my parents and my *kaka kaki* took care of me. But she was regular in sending money back home,' she said.

Reminiscing about Murmu's participation in a drama competition, she was all praise for her artistic expertise.

> She was the protagonist of a play called *Jivi Jharna* opposite a girl named Parbati Kisku, which was directed by dramatist Gobinda Soren. She was exceptional in playing her role. She was equally good at music and dance. I also realize now that the hours she spent reading books are bearing fruit now as I hear her speak so well on all issues, be it about the country, its culture, religion or women's empowerment. She has learnt a lot from her life and from people around her.

She admitted that she never thought Murmu would lead the country one day. She said:

> She was the protagonist of many dramas, but I never thought she would be the lead player running the country. Let alone president, I never imagined she would become a minister or a governor. She was so soft-spoken and straightforward, besides being simple, that it was difficult to fathom that she could learn it all as and when responsibilities fell on her.

Soren retired from her job after completing her full tenure. She had consistently been in touch with Murmu ever since her school days. She met Murmu after the latter won her first election in 2000 in the BJD–BJP alliance government in Odisha. She recalled:

> I was so pleasantly surprised to see her being elevated to the post of commerce and transport minister. We had organized a felicitation ceremony in her honour at the Soochana Bhavan in 2003. She was on the dais but the moment the event was over, she came down to meet me and bowed to me in front of everyone. For her I was 'Didi' and she had tremendous respect for me. She was filled with humility and respect for everyone.

Soren added, 'I was never made to sit in the waiting lounge, she had instructed her people to let me in to wherever she was in the house. She would also cook a variety of food on her own and feed us all.'

Murmu was a foodie and loved non-vegetarian dishes. Not only did she relish good food, she also cooked a lot for others. Sweets were her favourite. Some say that this sweet tooth of hers continues even today, though she has been vegetarian for the past few years.

While staying in hotels during her political visits to Bhubaneswar, there have been many times that she called up Soren and asked her to prepare food for her. 'She did not like hotel or circuit house food much. I would make a good number of dishes for her and she would visit to relish all those,' remembered Soren.

Prodding her on Murmu's contribution to the Adivasi community led Soren to narrate one incident after another. She fondly recollected:

> Her contribution to the Santali language getting into the Eighth Schedule of the Constitution is immense.

We celebrate Santali Dibas on 22 December every year. The day Santali was included in the Eighth Schedule of the Constitution, we all danced in a hall in the RBI colony auditorium here in Bhubaneswar. She has done a lot for the language and she too danced on that day. I remember it was 22 December 2004. Similarly, we have a Santali women's association called Rajgal Jaher Aayo Mahila Samiti, which organized a meet and invited her and she eagerly agreed to come. She made me share the dais with her that day.

This samiti that had more than a hundred members then has now thinned, with most fellow members retiring from service and leaving for their native places.

Soren also attributes the establishment of the Jaher in Niladri Vihar, Bhubaneswar, to Murmu. After a lot of persuasion, the home department allotted a space for the construction of Jaher boundary in 2009. 'Chaitanya Prasad Majhi was the minister in the BJD government and the present Chhattisgarh governor Biswabhusan Harichandan came to install a statue of Pandit Raghunath Murmu, the originator of Ol Chiki script. Chief Minister Naveen Patnaik inaugurated it; Murmu played a big role in all this. She pursued the matter strongly,' explained Soren, who has been with Murmu even during her difficult phases.

'Putti is affable and affectionate,' Soren stated. This same simplicity, she explained, became her biggest strength in her later political career, as it made her dear to political opponents too. She met Murmu during her debut visit to Odisha immediately following her presidential election. They exchanged pleasantries at the Raj Bhavan on 10 November 2022, and Soren promised to visit her in Rashtrapati Bhavan soon.

3
A Wife and Teacher: Marriage, Children and People

Delha Soren was the person who introduced Murmu and Shyam Charan, the man whom she would go on to marry.

He was posted in Puri as divisional accounts officer. Describing the circumstances in which he met Murmu, Soren said that Shyam Charan used to visit her office in Bhubaneswar. They knew each other as colleagues, and it was through Soren that Shyam Charan met Murmu during one of his visits to Soren's quarters. She recalled:

> He took a liking towards Murmu after they met at the house we were staying in. He wanted to propose marriage to Murmu and I advised him to meet her father in their village. Since their villages were a few kilometres away, and they belonged to the same community, I found it to be a common thing to take the liking forward to a lifelong relationship. Everything happened in the way usually an arranged marriage happens. Shyam Charan certainly took Murmu seriously to make her his life partner, which happened a little later.

In 1980, Shyam Charan had already joined a nationalized bank as an officer. He was the only son of his mother and had four sisters. The family stayed together in Pahadpur, near Balabhadrapur, a few kilometres from the national highway to Rairangpur. After getting to know Murmu, he really wanted to marry her and decided to take the proposal to her family as per Soren's advice. Along with some relatives, he went to Uparbeda to meet Biranchi Narayan Tudu. As discussions proceeded, Shyam Charan could sense Tudu's reluctance regarding the proposal. However, he persisted in his efforts to convince Tudu. But Tudu remained adamant and refused him.

Murmu's sister-in-law Sakramani Tudu (wife of her brother Taranisen Tudu) confirmed that the marriage was solemnized after many initial ups and downs.[1] After Tudu's initial refusal, Shyam Charan remained in her village for a couple of days and tried convincing his future father-in-law. Since Sakramani married into the Tudu family much later, she said that she has heard the story from many people in the family and village about how difficult it was for Shyam Charan to make Tudu agree to the proposal.

In spite of knowing that Shyam Charan was the only son in his family, well settled, good natured and belonging to the same community, Tudu did not relent. Shyam Charan also had land in Pahadpur and the family was well to do. He was the only one who earned in the family.

Villagers in Uparbeda said that Tudu was not keen on the

---

[1] 'President-Elect Draupadi Murmu's Sister-in-Law Shares Unheard Tale of Early Life,' YouTube, https://bit.ly/406O0iA. Accessed on 14 March 2023. Also from interviews conducted by the author between 29 December 2022 and 20 January 2023.

proposal, as Murmu had only been working for a year and he did not want her to leave the job. Others felt that it was natural for a girl's father to throw tantrums when any family comes asking for the daughter's hand in a Santali family. It is usually the groom's family that has to make the first move and convince the bride's family to agree to the marriage.

After much coaxing for almost seven days, Tudu eventually agreed to the marriage, on the condition that Shyam Charan would have to give an ox, a bull and sixteen saris to Murmu's family at the time of the wedding. The Santali rituals also warrant the groom to pay a dowry to the bride's family if he wishes to solemnize the marriage. Shyam Charan agreed and the marriage took place. Droupadi Tudu became Droupadi Murmu.

'It was an arranged marriage. However, both had known each other for some time before tying the knot. He had a good job, but maybe Biranchi Narayan did not want Murmu to compromise on her job that was feeding the family,' said Soren, echoing the ideas of the villagers. 'I felt he was apprehensive regarding whether Murmu would continue to take care of him and their family after marriage or stop due to some pressure.'

After the marriage, Murmu shifted to a different house in Shastri Nagar close to Unit 4. Soren, too, got married in the meantime and shifted to a separate residence.

MARRIED LIFE

While Murmu continued to work in Bhubaneswar, Shyam Charan moved to different places as his was a transferable job as a Bank of India officer. He used to travel to and from Bhubaneswar frequently, and his sisters too started staying with Murmu in Bhubaneswar for months. During this period, Soren was blessed with a son. She remembered having invited Murmu and her family to attend the child's birthday, which Murmu attended when she was pregnant with her first child. It has been a characteristic trait of Murmu to remain as social as possible. She has always made it a point to attend as many events as possible and goes to all functions for which she had invitations.

In a few months, she delivered a baby girl, and that was when Soren felt Murmu had to juggle between her house in Pahadpur, job in Bhubaneswar and taking care of the newborn. She never wanted to leave her job, but pressure was mounting on her from her in-laws. 'My in-laws did not want me to continue the job as it took a lot of time and they felt I was unable to devote time to the family. I was under pressure to quit the job,' she remembered.[2]

People close to Murmu said that she was a perfect amalgamation of a caring daughter, daughter-in-law and efficient working woman. A few villagers in Pahadpur said that during the 1980s, when working women were few, despite being a government servant, Murmu never had any issues doing the household chores that a daughter-in-law is expected to do in rural areas. 'She would cook, sweep, rear goat and also fetch fodder for the cattle whenever she was in Pahadpur. Her mother-in-law never treated her as special. So whatever she was expected to do, she did without any complaints or regrets,' said Miska Murmu, a Pahadpur villager who stayed close by and saw Murmu become a member of Shyam Charan's family.

---

[2] 'Dr Itirani Samanta in Conversation with Droupadi Murmu' (Video in Odia), YouTube, http://bit.ly/3Jrdhib. Accessed on 9 March 2023.

Murmu had three more children in subsequent years, and it started getting very difficult for her to manage the children and travel to Bhubaneswar and back. By then, Shyam Charan was posted at a bordering village in the district. So, be it Pahadpur or Bhubaneswar, Murmu had to manage it all on her own. Shuttling between two places was getting difficult by the day. Additionally, her eldest child, who was three years old by then, had started falling sick frequently.

In and out of hospitals because of her ailments, despite treatments, the girl was not showing any signs of recovery. There was a point in time when she had to be hospitalized for months together, as doctors treating her suspected that she was suffering from meningitis. Such was the situation that Murmu, who was not one to take leave unless necessary, started staying away from office. Her daughter's treatment continued for months, but she could not survive. And that became another turning point in Murmu's career.

The child's death was like the final nail in the coffin. She was asked by her in-laws to quit her job and stay with the family in Rairangpur. But Murmu had also promised her father to take care of her parents and siblings. So she discussed her desire to continue her job with Shyam Charan, which enabled her to care for them.

Shyam Charan was a senior officer in the Bank of India, so her leaving the job did not have a great impact on the family's finances. He was understanding and always supported Murmu, according to Nabin Kumar Ram, district BJP working body member, three-time councillor of Rairangpur and a close confidant of Murmu. It would not be wrong to say that he was her man Friday and has been with her since 1997, when she first contested the councillor election on a BJP ticket.

After losing a child, she finally stopped going to Bhubaneswar in 1983, giving due respect to Shyam Charan's and his mother's feelings. She, however, did not resign formally. The prolonged leave from office without notice finally must have been taken as her resignation. She travelled with Shyam Charan wherever he was posted, but not for long because, in a few years, he was posted in Rairangpur and the family stayed together in the town.

When the Murmus moved to Rairangpur in 1994, they initially lived in a rented accommodation in ward number 2. The house was owned by another Bank of India official who was a resident of Baripada. When the officer shifted to Baripada after a long stint in Rairangpur, he wanted to sell off the house, and the Murmus bought it. The place is named Baidaposi, and it is situated on Mahuldiha Road. This house has been a witness to Murmu's elevation from teacher to councillor, MLA, minister, governor and now the president. It has also seen the worst times of the Murmu family.

After deciding to stay back with the family in Rairangpur, Murmu called her mother, Singo, and brothers, Bhagat and Tarinisen, to stay with her, as her father was no more. She wanted to take care of them. It also helped Murmu, as her children were under her mother's care while her brother Tarinisen and his wife looked after the house. They continue to stay with Murmu till date, while Bhagat's son and daughter-in-law, Dulari, are residents of Uparbeda.

TEACHING BEGINS

With the children growing up, Murmu got ample time at home after all three of them left for school. Even Shyam

Charan did not want her to remain at home if she could work somewhere close by. He also knew Murmu was not happy whiling away time at home. The couple discussed the matter and decided to talk to people at the nearby school—Sri Aurobindo Integral Education and Research Centre, the only English-medium school in the town—about whether she could teach there. It was a school that could only function as a part of the Sri Aurobindo study circle. It was also close to their house. She felt that working there could keep her busy and also give her an opportunity to teach, which was close to her heart. She has always attributed her success in life to the strong foundation laid by teachers in her school and college. She, too, wanted to invest in the future of hundreds of students.[3]

Rabindra Patnaik, one of the members of the Sri Aurobindo study circle, which was established in 1949, said:

> In 1993, I was a member of school management committee of Sri Aurobindo Integral Education and Research Centre. I was simultaneously working in Bank of India, Rairangpur. Shyam Charan and I were colleagues for a long time and shared the same room in the office. He once asked me if there was any prospect of Madam Murmu getting an opportunity to teach at the school. He was very honest when he said she has a lot of time and as she has left one job already, she would be happy to teach at the school.

The then secretary of the school management committee, Anadi Shankar Pani, was also a Bank of India employee, and

---

[3] 'President Droupadi Murmu's Address | National Teacher's Day 2022,' YouTube, http://bit.ly/3Ld9MwV. Accessed on 10 March 2023.

he and Patnaik discussed Murmu's appointment. 'We had met Madam Murmu many times as a Bank of India staffer's family member, but we had not thought of her as a teacher. However, we decided to go for the recruitment and asked Shyam babu to send an application to the school showing keenness to work as a teacher,' recollected Patnaik.

Soon, an application in Odia reached them, and without any other formalities, an appointment letter was issued. Since Murmu had clearly stated her intention of teaching on honorary basis, there was no mention of any salary for the job. 'The only thing she agreed to take from the school was the rickshaw fare she would have to pay to commute daily,' smiled Patnaik.

That marked another turning point in Murmu's career. Her tryst with teaching began in 1994 and continued till 1997.

With the motive of strengthening the foundation of students, she expressed her desire to teach the youngest of all children—lower and higher kindergarten students of the institute. The classes for these children were conducted in a large classroom with two blackboards on either end. The classroom measured about 15 feet by 12 feet, and Patnaik said that it continues to be known by her name even years after she left.

Within no time, Murmu became the favourite teacher of the students and was considered hard working. Her way of teaching created a benchmark for others to follow. She was never hard on her students even when they faltered. Rather, she chose to make them understand the nuances of the subject she was teaching through love and affection. Reminiscing his time with Murmu in the school, Patnaik said that she won the hearts of all students. No one ever saw her getting angry or irritated under any circumstance. She was immune to anything around her because her goal was different—to make good citizens.

'She was greatly inspired by Sri Ma Anandamayi and Sri Aurobindo,' Patnaik said. Murmu narrated her feelings for the institution during her maiden speech after taking over as the president. Driven by the philosophy of the two spiritual leaders who have influenced her, Murmu mentioned the school in her speech and congratulated it for completing 150 years of existence.[4]

Patnaik also mentioned how Murmu remembered the birthdays of her students in the class and never forgot to wish them. Her love for work made her a unique personality. It did not take her long to create an identity for herself. In spite of being known as Mrs Shyam Charan Murmu for a long time, she was able to create an identity as the most sincere teacher of Sri Aurobindo School very quickly, according to Patnaik.

During the Republic Day and Independence Day parades, she was the one to lead the students to the ground and personally taught them to sing and dance so that they could perform in front of a large gathering. 'Her sincerity is unparalleled. I don't remember her taking leave at all unless she was really unwell. She would be the first one to reach the school ahead of all other teachers. These are some of the qualities that have brought her this far,' said Patnaik with a sense of pride at having known her up close.

Murmu often gave examples of President Radhakrishnan and asked students to follow in his footsteps to reach the

---

[4]"Full Text of Draupadi Murmu's Maiden Speech as President', *OneIndia*, 25 July 2022, https://bit.ly/3y7FAM1. Accessed on 3 March 2023.

top. She has now gone on to become Dr Radhakrishnan's real follower of high principles and morals.

She never refused to teach anyone. If a student wanted to clear their doubts, she would teach them even at home. 'She made everyone feel important and loved, respected all and always sported a smile. She has also not forgotten to attribute credit to the school that gave her an identity,' Patnaik said, remembering her oath-taking speech where she mentioned how the school shaped her sensibility.

Patnaik and his wife rushed to meet Murmu after her name was declared as the presidential candidate just before she left Rairangpur for Bhubaneswar. He remembers that amid tight security, she asked her security personnel to allow the couple to meet her. They spoke, and Murmu promised to visit the school sometime soon. He has preserved some of the pictures clicked with Murmu on 21 June 2022 as his prized possessions.

The principal of the school, Pramila Swain, was all praise for Murmu. She said:

> Her sincerity and punctuality have been examples for all teachers. Her life motto is even more inspiring. We have a lot to learn from her life and career. She never lost her cool and knew how to motivate children. She made the students understand with love what many others failed to do. I remember she used to carry chocolates to reward students who answered well in her class.[5]

Sushil Kumar Das, the founder–principal of the school, whom Murmu called 'principal guru', is no more, but

---

[5] 'School Remembers "Teacher Droupadi Murmu" as She Takes Oath 1,400 km Away,' *NDTV*, http://bit.ly/428maV3. Accessed on 14 March 2023.

people in his family vouch for Murmu's respect for Das till date. Patnaik remembered how, one day in 2017, while she was in the district during her gubernatorial tenure, he reminded her that it was Das's birthday. He said:

> I knew she was here so I informed her personal assistant about Principal Guru's birthday on Snana Purnima. The moment I informed Madam Murmu, she defied all protocol to meet him at his house. She carried an *uttariya* and flowers for Principal Guru, stopped by his house and paid her respects to him.[6] Those were the days when her name was doing the rounds for the presidential elections, and she sought his blessings. Das blessed her, assuring that she will certainly become the president one day. Today, he is no more, but I am sure Madam must remember him for blessing her.

She gave her colleagues and other co-workers enough reasons to emulate her behaviour and conduct. That is why she was always looked upon with awe—her ability to withstand any adverse situation was her trump card. Guardians of Murmu's students said they never had to worry about the subjects she taught. The students scored more than 70 per cent in her class and that, for Murmu, was the highest award. The guardians adored her for being the perfect teacher and respected her for the social work she was committed to.[7]

Murmu was the favourite of students and parents. People who were dissatisfied with the quality of education in the school roped in private tutors, but in Murmu's case, that

---

[6]An uttariya is a special cloth that is given to people as a mark of respect.
[7]'Tejasvani: Guest Draupadi Murmu, Governor of Jharkhand,' YouTube, https://bit.ly/3kY7oQb. Accessed on 10 March 2023

was never required. Madhumati Padhiary, who was working in a bank in the town, said:

> I remember she taught social studies but my children never felt the need to go for extra classes or tuitions privately as they understood her subjects pretty well. The best thing about her tenure in the school is she remembered every student by name and also us parents. During interactions at the beginning of the school day or when classes ended, she would brief me about how my children were performing in the class.[8]

Both of Padhiary's children, now settled in multinational companies, fondly remember Murmu.

Similar views were also expressed by Shakuntala Behera, who was Murmu's neighbour. Behera claims that apart from being affectionate, Murmu was a social person and interacted with everyone in the neighbourhood. Behera, whose daughter is currently a bank officer in Mumbai, said:

> We never thought a simple teacher and neighbour of ours will become the president of the country. At least I did not see any such indication other than of course her humaneness. She won elections but never showed off or boasted about anything. She was social in nature and visited our house any time we invited her for an event. At home, she was like any good neighbour. My daughter was her student and she was very fond of Murmu. She never missed her class and was in awe of her as a teacher. Today as she remembers Murmu, she swells in pride for being her student.[9]

---

[8] Quote from an interview conducted by the author on 27 December 2022
[9] Quote from an interview conducted by the author on 15 December 2022

Murmu's daughter Itishree said that while studying in the same school that her mother taught in, she was under pressure as a student and daughter. Her friends also expressed their fear of her mother, as she was the only teacher who conducted surprise tests.

As a mother, Murmu instilled discipline in her children. Itishree remembered, 'She used to get angry with us when we watched TV for hours and always stressed the need for studies and the importance of a career. She encouraged me to go to Pune for higher studies and never discriminated between me and my brothers.'[10] Itishree studied in Pune at the Suryadatta Institute of Management and Mass Communication while both her brothers completed their education in Bhubaneswar.

SERVICE BEFORE POLITICS

Murmu never needed a reason to meet people. On any given day, she would go around and help those in need. Because she was well read and kept abreast of the issues affecting the people in the region, she would volunteer to help many people. This earned her a good name as someone who was dedicated to the cause of humanity.

Between 1994 and 1997, she was associated with many civil society organizations and went on to become the president and vice president of many committees, such as Adivasi Social Educational and Cultural Association (ASECA) and school governing bodies. She participated in the ASECA's motto of uplifting the less privileged and the

---

[10]Singha, Minati, 'Mom's Hard Work, Integrity Have Taken Her to Where She Is Today, Says Droupadi Murmu's Daughter,' *The Times of* India, 24 June 2022, https://bit.ly/3YhNFZf. Accessed on 3 March 2023.

marginalized. Villages in the vicinity of the town spoke of how Murmu, through her social activism, helped them get land *patta*s (records) that had been pending for years.

In spite of working at school and home, Murmu would take time out of her schedule to attend meetings organized by various sociocultural organizations. Nabin Kumar Ram stated:

> She endeared herself to the people to an extent through her work and also the way she spoke. Being learned, she knew many things that many did not know, and people would therefore want her to be a part of their organizations. She has always been a people's person, and everyone around her agrees that she religiously worked for social causes much before taking a plunge into elections or politics. She would take part in various awareness drives and cultural programmes and contribute by way of organizing or garnering more support. These things made her a popular face among the public in the town.[11]

Ram added, 'Not many know that Murmu's inclination to serve the people was so intense that she contested the council elections in 1992 as an independent candidate but lost.' Murmu still continues to mention that serving people becomes a little more impactful as a people's representative in comparison to a normal citizen. This is why, even after her term as the governor, she wanted the BJP membership again so that she could serve people in a better way.[12]

---

[11]All quotes by Nabin Kumar Ram are from an interview conducted by the author on 27 December 2022.
[12]'Exclusive Interview with Former Governor of Jharkhand, Draupadi Murmu', YouTube, https://bit.ly/3T8MhXN. Accessed on 10 March 2023.

A Wife and Teacher: Marriage, Children and People

Ram, recollecting how every party wanted to field her as their candidate for the council elections in 1997, stated:

> She contested the 1992 Notified Area Council elections for the post of councillor in ward number 2, but I can't say what the driving force behind the intent was. But once she contested, she was in the eyes of the political parties. Since then our party, the Bharatiya Janata Party, had kept a close watch on her. We wanted to tap her potential by making her agree to contest the next elections with a BJP ticket.

In 1997, however, she did not show much enthusiasm for elections, according to Ram. When ward number 2 became reserved for an SC/ST woman candidate, her name came to the forefront, as she was a well-educated Adivasi woman who was known as a good teacher and human being.

Rabindra Nath Mohanta, then BJP district president of Mayurbhanj, had been staying close to the school back then and knew Shyam Charan pretty well. He had often noticed Murmu's work and the way she dealt with people, including the parents of her students. Not only that, he also appreciated her participation in social organizations in and around Rairangpur. The way she got along with people was reflected in her strong public standing even in those days. He wanted someone like her to be a part of the BJP and contest the council election that year. 'He, I believe, is the initiator of Murmu into politics,' reminisced Ram. Mohanta had earlier been the chairman of Bijatola block in the Mayurbhanj district, Odisha, as the Swatantra Party candidate.

Rajkishore Das, the present BJD MLA from Morada, was also contesting the election for the post of chairman as a

BJP candidate for Rairangpur NAC in 1997. Many said that Das was insistent on Murmu contesting the election to the council that year.

Ram explained Murmu's prospective candidature:

> During that period, since the BJP was looking for a candidate for the councillor post, we wanted an Adivasi female face who would work dedicatedly for the cause of the people, someone who had an understanding of people's issues in a tribal dominated district like Mayurbhanj. Didi seemed to be the perfect candidate. She was popular among the town residents and had a clean image as a teacher. Her way of conduct was noticeably different from others'. Didi was respected by everyone as a teacher. Almost everyone who knew her saw her to be the most uncomplicated and well-behaved person. She had a niche identity as a teacher and social worker and that worked.

Apart from her qualifications and social standing, another reason why she was being looked at as a prospective candidate was her uncle, Kartik Majhi, was the Swatantra Party MLA and minister in the R.N. Singh Deo ministry. Majhi was the one who had facilitated Murmu's admission to the Government Girls High School in Bhubaneswar. Since he was a family member and already a big name in politics, it was generally taken as an indication that Murmu would take to politics like a fish takes to water.

Murmu, the BJP knew, had felt an affiliation towards their party for a long time. She was a follower of the then PM Atal Behari Vajpayee and his ideologies. She was also impressed by the party workers who went to people and worked door-to-door to serve them.[13]

Both Mohanta and Das met Shyam Charan and expressed their desire to make Murmu the councillor candidate. The Congress and JMM, which were active in the bordering areas, also approached her through Shyam Charan in 1987, since he was deeply interested in politics himself. Everyone knew that Murmu would agree to fight the election only if she was convinced that she would be able to make a valuable contribution or if Shyam Charan was able to persuade her.

In the meantime, many BJP supporters and workers also tried speaking to Murmu directly to contest the elections as the party candidate. They convinced her to enter the fray in the larger interest of people in the Adivasi-dominated district, according to Patnaik.

In a small place like Rairangpur, where even working as a teacher was not easily acceptable, getting into politics, she feared, would not be taken well.[14] This was especially so because she belonged to the Adivasi community, which was not open to women stepping out of home; joining politics would mean inviting trouble from her own people more than adversaries. Murmu was apprehensive that her community would not look at politics with respect and she might have to face backlash.

A few years ago, in an interview on Doordarshan, Murmu said:

---

[13]'Discussion with Former Governor of Jharkhand Draupadi Murmu', YouTube, http://bit.ly/3l7aKAr. Accessed on 14 March 2023.
[14]'Tejasvani: Guest Draupadi Murmu, Governor of Jharkhand', YouTube, https://bit.ly/3kY7oQb. Accessed on 10 March 2023.

> I was not sure if I would succeed in contesting the NAC elections. One thing was sure that if I take up some work, I complete it with dedication. So if I take the plunge, I would not want to be a stamp paper councillor, neither did I want to get into the party fold for no reason. I wanted to work for people.[15]

People were not open to accepting the Adivasi community women working outside the confines of the home, according to Murmu.

However, Das knew that Shyam Charan had no objection to Murmu contesting. They were waiting for her to agree to contest the elections from the party. He recalls:

> She was educated and had all the qualities that would make her stand out in the crowd. It was rare to find an Adivasi woman who was educated, deeply rooted to the community's culture and tradition and at the same time liked by all. And we did not have a single Adivasi in the party who the population could identify with. I knew I have got the right person to contest the NAC elections.[16]

Ram added, 'In those days, when men took all the decisions of the family, we thought it wise to go through Shyam babu instead of directly approaching Didi. So before Raju bhai (Rajkishore Das) came to bell the cat, we set the tone by discussing everything with Shyam babu.'

Since Das was responsible for candidate selection for the BJP, it was he who was expected to do the talking with

---

[15]Ibid.
[16]All quotes by Rajkishore Das are from an interview conducted by the author on 12 November 2022.

Murmu. But he too was in a dilemma on how to approach her. He shared:

> I was worried, but I had to make the first move if I wanted the right candidate. I approached Murmu and explained to her why the party wanted her to contest the elections. I knew there would be resistance and hesitation, and that happened. She was not convinced because belonging to the Adivasi Santal community and coming out to fight elections were diametrically opposite then. We wanted her to join us and assured her that the party would give her the scope for growth. And if she was voted in, even the tribal majority could look towards a bright future.

He also recollected Shyam Charan's contribution in the whole issue. 'He was a fine gentleman. He told me he had no qualms about his wife contesting the elections. He left it completely to Murmu to decide whether she would join politics or not,' he narrated.

As Murmu has said, women from families of politicians, those from urban societies or those who were highly educated, such as Nandini Satapathy, Indira Gandhi and Sarojini Naidu, were welcomed into politics. Their backgrounds were different from Santals and Adivasis in general. Getting into politics was, therefore, a call that was very difficult for Murmu to take. It was Shyam Charan's insistence, the party's interest and backing plus the motivation of serving people that made her say yes.[17]

---

[17]'Dr Itirani Samanta in Conversation with Droupadi Murmu' (Video in Odia), YouTube, http://bit.ly/3Jrdhib. Accessed on 9 March 2022.

Finally, Murmu decided, albeit in the last hour, to file her nomination from the BJP ticket. This marked her entry into active politics, a trajectory that eventually led to her presidential role a little more than two decades later.

4

The One with No Peer: On-Ground Legislation

Murmu joined the BJP in 1997 and contested Rairangpur NAC elections, which was when her political career kickstarted.

On the day she filed her nomination papers for the Rairangpur NAC elections, she was aware that she had a large support base, particularly among the teaching community and guardians of her students.[1] Her nature had endeared her to people from all quarters.

Though the BJP did not have much sway in the district back then, with the Congress and the JMM holding majority of the seats, the BJP workers, with the support of the Rashtriya Swayamsevak Sangh (RSS), had started forming a base by getting involved in social work and helping people from all walks of life. They went door-to-door, seeking people's support and, in the process, also resolved their concerns. They offered rice, food, clothes and other requisites to people who needed a livelihood, according to Nabin Kumar Ram. Murmu, who was a grassroots worker and had seen the party workers slog day in and out, could

---

[1]"Tejasvani: Guest Draupadi Murmu, Governor of Jharkhand,' YouTube, http://bit.ly/3JJZBis. Accessed on 16 March 2023.

feel a sense of belonging with them.

Meanwhile, after Murmu confirmed her participation in the elections as a BJP candidate, she filed her nomination and got down to campaigning. She was soon seen on posters and walls, but was already in the hearts of the people.

For days on end, she would go campaigning with other members of the party and meet lakhs of people who already knew her as a teacher and social worker. Her affinity to the cause of the people made her stand out. She did not limit herself to ward number 2, which she was representing, but went around all the wards speaking to people, spending time with them and sharing food. Accompanying her were her supporters and the party's district leaders, including Rajkishore Das and Ram.

Finally, the elections took place and the results came out soon after: Murmu was declared the winner, and the party celebrated. It was the first dent the party made in the tribal-dominated region. For Murmu, too, it was the first election of her life that she won—she was voted as the councillor of ward number 2 of Rairangpur NAC. In a few days, she was also elected the vice chairperson of the NAC while Das remained the chairman.

She attributed her victory in the councillor elections to teachers and guardians of ward number 2 along with thousands of people who had trusted her, supported her and showered much love and affection on her. She also expressed her gratitude to the party for giving her the opportunity to do something for the people.

ON GROUND: CREATING NEW IDENTITIES

Within no time, the diligent Murmu was seen working on ground in the wards for various developmental and sanitation issues. She started her supervisory role by ensuring that the NAC turned clean and green and initiated action in the areas where sanitation was in shambles. Before that, nothing had been undertaken. Cleanliness and the drainage clearance system had been neglected in Rairangpur, and they became her priority. She started personally monitoring every area under her jurisdiction. For days on end, she would stand along the roads and drains and supervise the cleanliness drives. She never had any qualms about standing alongside sweepers and cleaners and instructing them. Her work led to a visible change in the town and garnered appreciation from everyone. Ram stated that every insider knew she had the ability to shine and would go all out to work for the betterment of the people. 'We had seen Didi work in many places much before she contested. So it did not come as a surprise for us that she was a devoted worker,' he said.

Since she used to walk or take a rickshaw to reach her destinations every day, Shyam Charan gifted her a Maruti 800 car to facilitate her movement to places and supervise the work. With the car, she was able to access distant places with greater ease and save a lot of time, which allowed her to work more. Recently, while addressing a meeting, she spoke about her tenure as the councillor and how one must respect any work one does or others do. There was a time when women were not considered fit for politics or elections, but she stood her ground. After her victory, she never felt bad about standing for hours with sweepers and cleaning staff throughout the town. That term in the NAC gave her the much-needed confidence to take on bigger responsibilities. She believes that no work is big or small, bad or good. Duty is god and work is worship.[2]

She was the first one to work for a swachh Rairangpur, much before the Swachh Bharat campaign was launched in the country in 2014. Her efficiency left a mark on the town, from common people to political supporters and adversaries. 'I became associated with Didi during the NAC election and was always with her through thick and thin. I have seen her way of working,' said Ram. 'She put her heart in whatever she did, and you rarely find such people. Some other party members and I always ensured that we were with her every day when she went about her rounds in the town. She indeed brought transformations in the town.'

In a few years, the town got a distinctively new identity. And Murmu got hers. Halfway through her tenure, the 2000 General Election was declared. Her term as the councillor, which should have continued till 2002, came to an abrupt end when the party decided to make her the MLA candidate for Rairangpur constituency. Though she was not prepared for this proposal, people from across the town as well as party members assured her of their support.

Das remembered:

> The party had its candidate for the constituency, as that year, it became a reserved seat for women ST candidates. So the party, without any second thoughts, knew that it was for Murmu. She fit the bill, and she

---

[2]"Tour Villages and Study Government Schemes, President Advises Students,' *Outlook*, 5 December 2022, https://bit.ly/3SHetB3. Accessed on 3 March 2023.

had also gained experience in the public sphere as the vice chairperson of the NAC. Her work was noticeable and behaviour praiseworthy. Everyone wanted her to contest and we knew we would win.

Ram mentioned Advocate Rabindra Mohanta, who was the first one to identify Murmu's potential and recommend her name for the NAC polls. 'Mohanta Babu had always seen Didi being active in social life and eliciting the respect of the people all around her. He was very influential in the BJP circle, as he had won the Bijatola seat earlier. He recommended Didi's name to us for the Rairangpur assembly constituency,' he said.

MAKING A MARK: LEGISLATOR

Murmu was not worried about the election or its results. She never shied away from taking on bigger responsibilities. Her concern was only one: If she became an MLA, it would be much more demanding than working as a councillor. But she allayed her fears after much thought and multiple discussions with her husband as well as party members and agreed to contest for the Rairangpur Assembly seat.

In those days, politics was considered an out-and-out male-dominated field, where women were hardly seen working alongside various kinds of people day and night. Becoming a people's representative meant being devoted to the people more than one's family. Unsure if she could take this responsibility, staying away from her home and children to attend meetings, she fought with her own thoughts—that's how people close to her explained Murmu's mental state back then.

In a Doordarshan interview, which was recorded during her term as the governor, she said:

> As councillor, I knew I could stay back in the town and come back home at night to take care of my children, but I was unsure about what would happen if I get elected as an MLA. When I thought aloud my fears, I got all the support of the party members, who assured me that everything will be taken care of. They said they will support me in any work I would take up. Even my husband agreed to be with me in every situation. So I consented.[3]

As electioneering began in full swing, Murmu's days and nights were spent among the thousands of people she met every day in every village under the Rairangpur Assembly constituency. That was the year when the BJD and the BJP in Odisha decided to go to polls in an alliance with a mutual seat-sharing agreement. The BJP had, by then, created a dent in the tribal-dominated district and the Rairangpur seat was reserved for an ST woman candidate, while the BJD had no representation there.

In the same interview, Murmu further stated:

> I had a feeling that people with political clout are difficult to handle; some are rude while others have addiction to bad habits and it would be impossible for me to get along. But I never speak rudely, nor have I ever nurtured any addictive habits. I needed courage and, surprisingly, I never faced any wrong behaviour from any of my political associates or opponents.

---

[3] 'Tejasvani: Guest Draupadi Murmu, Governor of Jharkhand,' YouTube, http://bit.ly/3JJZBis. Accessed on 16 March 2023.

Her influence grew with time, particularly in rural areas. 'She was never the one to sit at home idle. She worked day and night, so it was natural that people reposed faith in her. Extensive travelling into the remotest of places, meeting hordes of people, mingling with them, listening to them and promising to redress their grievances are what made her a favourite of the masses,' said Ram.

Subsequently, elections were held in February 2000 and Murmu won the Rairangpur Assembly constituency seat. She got 25,110 votes, leaving behind Congress candidate Laxman Majhi, who had 20,542 votes. In the state, the BJD won sixty-eight seats while the BJP, its alliance partner, won thirty-eight. The Congress got twenty-six. Das explained:

> I had been associated very closely with her during her political journey in Odisha and I felt that Murmu had been working with her impeccable behaviour right from day one till date. She would never get irritated or angry; she had tremendous control over herself and knew how to manage party affairs extraordinarily well. I believe that these made her one of the most respected members of the party. She has earned goodwill and love from everyone. The best part is that she has never fallen prey to any kind of groupism because of her clean heart. She has been impartial to the core.

Post the 2000 elections, Murmu was chosen as a member of the Council of Ministers in the BJP–BJD coalition government in Odisha, first becoming the minister of state with independent charge for commerce and transport in March 2000 and then minister for fisheries and animal resources development from August 2002 to May 2004.

MINISTERSHIP

When the BJD–BJP alliance won, Naveen Patnaik was chosen to be the leader of the alliance and, thus, became the CM. It was time to select his Cabinet ministers. While leaders of the parties maintained that negotiation over the ministries was to be done mutually, Patnaik was certain about having a compact Cabinet, given the precarious condition of the state finances in 2000. On 2 March 2000, it was decided that a twenty-five-member Cabinet would be sworn in on 5 March. The BJD would have a share of sixteen while the BJP would get nine seats. Of the nine from the BJP, four people were likely to be included in the Cabinet while the remaining members were supposed to be ministers of state. Among the names doing the rounds for Cabinet ministers were leader of the BJP legislature party Biswabhusan Harichandan (currently the governor of Chhattisgarh), former party president Bimbadhar Kuanr, former minister Bed Prakash Agarwal and vice president of the party Prashanta Nanda. Besides these were two women for consideration as well—Droupadi Murmu and Nivedita Pradhan.

Since differences had cropped up within the alliance regarding the size of the ministry, CM Patnaik was ready to relax the size to thirty, if required. The BJP's demand for key portfolios, like home, rural development, panchayati raj and industry, also became a major bone of contention between the allies.

A BJP delegation, including Manmohan Samal, Jual Oram, Prasanna Mishra and Harichandan, had prepared a list of names to hand over to Patnaik at the meeting scheduled on 4 March.

Chotulal Mohanta, president of state working committee of the BJP, said:

> When we were traveling, I could see a pencil-scribbled list of probables and tried to get the names that were being carried by the team to Naveen Niwas for discussion. I was curious to know which portfolio they were looking at for Rairangpur MLA Murmu. Since most of the time we ended up getting textiles or SC/ST ministries, I could not help but ask Prasanna Mishra about the portfolio Didi was to get. But he did not wish to answer, though I proposed transport and commerce for her.

The BJP members who were in talks with the BJD were keen on the transport ministry because the Jamshola check gate in the district was the highest grosser among all toll gates in the state. 'We knew Didi might not handle the gate and its collections, but then there were party workers who would take care of these matters,' said Mohanta. The alliance partners deliberated till late in the night, even though the swearing-in ceremony was only a few hours away.

Finally, on 5 March, a twenty-five-member BJD–BJP coalition ministry took over with M.M. Rajendran, then governor of Odisha, administering the oath of office to all the ministers. Murmu was designated as the minister of state with independent charge of commerce and transport. That year, the Raj Bhavan was thrown open to the public to attend the swearing-in ceremony. Chief Minister Patnaik and A.U. Singh Deo, one of the ministers, took their respective oaths in English while rest of the ministers, including Murmu, took their oaths in Odia.

The day ushered in a new chapter in the life and career of Murmu. She stated:

> People, both men and women, normally misinterpret a woman's capability, and in my case, too, I could sense that when I took charge. They looked at me with a different lens, more so because I was an Adivasi woman. It was true that I had read about the ministries but had no idea about how the ministry functions, and transport department at that. But with time, I learnt the nitty-gritties, and with everyone's support, I performed pretty well in the department.[4]

The portfolio was surely a big responsibility for Murmu, a first-time minister who had no knowledge about how a department functions. She was told that the department collects money and is considered to be the revenue churner for the government. That development works are in no way related to the ministry was a shock for Murmu. 'Since the party lobbied for me to get the commerce and transport ministry, I was given the charge and I decided to give it my best shot,' Murmu reminisced.[5]

The first few months were a learning experience for Murmu. To understand the details of the ministry, she convened frequent meetings with the secretaries and other officials of the department and sat for hours to discuss issues pertaining to improving the department performance.

'We studied economics and political science in graduation and learnt the functioning of the ministry,

---

[4] 'An Exclusive Interview with India's First Tribal President, Draupadi Murmu by Dr. Itirani Samanta,' YouTube, http://bit.ly/420iZ1w. Accessed on 10 March 2023.
[5] Ibid.

but that was very different from the actual working of the government departments,' disclosed Murmu.[6] She was told that there were eighteen regional transport offices (RTOs) for thirty districts and twenty-three toll gates at different highways from where revenue was collected by RTOs and motor vehicle inspectors. It was the senior-level people from her own department who helped her understand its functioning.

To keep a track of all revenue collection from the check gates, she started convening quarterly meetings. These kept the officials on their toes. She was aware that the department was meant to earn revenue, and it did. 'But most of the money was flowing out the wrong way. Once I started taking updates, I found that the collection had grown much more than the previous years', earning us a lot of appreciation. Even CM Naveen Patnaik appreciated the department for good revenue collection,' said Murmu, who did not shy away from standing at the toll gates on many occasions to oversee collections.[7] Mohanta remembered:

> Didi was so daring that she did not mind going to the toll gates and standing there for hours to check if all was well. We would want her to sit in the car instead of standing under the sun, but she wouldn't listen. 'It is my work and I have to brave all odds to see the welfare of the department,' she would say.

However, Murmu loved being back in her constituency. She wanted to be among the people who had voted her to power. She wanted to work for them. Rairangpur, and

---

[6] Ibid.
[7] Ibid.

even the nearby areas, started getting a facelift with a wide range of development activities. Other than the days when she had meetings and assembly sessions, she would be in Rairangpur to devote time to her constituents.

Always present with her was her first personal assistant Satish Chandra Samal, who says Murmu never used to shudder at taking responsibilities, new or old. 'Grounded' was the word Samal used for Murmu's attitude throughout the four-year tenure he was attached to her. 'I have never seen her afraid or uncertain of anything related to her work. She took over the ministry without any knowledge of official processes, but she did not take more than two months to get a grasp on the proceedings,' Samal added. In the years he was with Murmu, he never felt like a subordinate—such was her relation with her department officials. He was also the one who spent most of the time in Rairangpur while travelling with Murmu. 'We would travel by overnight buses too,' he reminisced.[8]

He also said that ahead of the assembly session, she would prepare questions and answers as the department readied the statistics and data. 'There were nights when she would prepare her answers based on the department feedback and then present them the next day. Never once have I seen her taking leave or staying away from the secretariat or Assembly,' Samal reiterated.

Murmu, too, had spoken about her interest in getting involved with everything concerning her department in a media interview.[9] She would never lose an opportunity to

---

[8] All quotes by Satish Samal are from interviews conducted by the author on 28 December 2022 and 7 January 2023.
[9] 'Dr Itirani Samanta in Conversation with Droupadi Murmu' (Video in Odia), YouTube, http://bit.ly/3Jrdhib. Accessed on 9 March 2022.

respond to questions and neither would she allow anyone to point fingers at her when the Assembly was in session.

During her term as the commerce and transport minister, Murmu spent most of her local area development funds meant for development works in the constituency. Starting from constructing bridges on rivers and nullahs to laying roads and building temples and Jaher boundaries, she has done it all. Besides, the town now has dozens of club houses, which were built with Murmu's contribution. 'The bridge connecting Kaduani Chhak and Uparbeda was built during that phase between 2000 and 2004. Even electricity connections and roads were laid to most villages in the constituency,' Ram narrated, adding that an additional RTO was also established in the town.

TRANSPORTATION: DEBACLE AND PROGRESS

During this period, the Orissa State Commercial Transport Corporation (OSCTC) was in the red and had been disbanded. Employees were retrenched en masse, leading to unrest all over the state. Their plight was miserable, as they had no source of income and their families were squatting on the roads. A large number of people sat on a dharna. The Employees' Union of the OSCTC appealed to CM Patnaik to revive the corporation or redeploy the employees.

On 13 May 2000, then Public Enterprise Minister Bed Prakash Agarwal and Commerce and Transport Minister Murmu appealed to the new government through a memorandum to the CM to either merge the OSCTC with Orissa Mining Corporation or to make it a subsidiary unit of the latter. The memorandum stated that the OSCTC incurred losses primarily due to the failure of the integrated scheme introduced when the OSCTC had just taken off. That is why the then state government decided to revive it in a high-level meeting in 1986. However, as revival plans could not materialize, the government recommended its closure in 1997.

In a memorandum, the general secretary of the employees' union, Raghu Arakshit Sinha, said that with 300 idle employees and existing infrastructure, the disbanded corporation must be revived.

The union urged the CM to look into the matter immediately and fix a date for discussion. At least the retrenched employees could be given alternative employment opportunities, Sinha appealed.

Soon, funds were pumped into the corporation to make it stand on its own feet. The OSCTC became Orissa State Road Transport Corporation (OSRTC) and went through a major internal restructuring. From a bus-to-staff ratio of almost 1:18 in 1977–78, it became 1:4 in 2015–16 by overcoming the problem of overstaffing. Murmu's contribution in all this was immense.

The OSRTC also received accolades for lowest operational cost under the mofussil category for two consecutive years, 2002–03 and 2003–04, by the Association of State Road Transport Undertakings. Later, it received the transport minister's trophy for safe transport lowest accident record for the years 2004–05 and 2005–06 from the Ministry of Road Transport and Highways.

The government was committed to formulating a pro-people policy keeping in view the hardships of the rural and poor people. It was then contemplating computerizing transport management and ticket and regional transport offices. Murmu assured that an assistance of ₹300 crore had been sought from the Centre to revamp the transport sector. This included assistance for computerization of RTOs and the twenty-three check gates of the state.[10] She also sought assistance for deploying cranes and ambulances on the national highways to meet exigencies during accidents. Besides, seeking support for setting up eight more pollution checking centres was also on the cards.

The then Rajya Sabha member and BJP president Manmohan Samal told the media that it was decided at a BJD–BJP coordination meeting to initiate the withdrawal of cases lodged against bus owners under the Essential Services Maintenance Act during various strikes that occurred rampantly in those days.

In the meantime, the private bus owners had been regularly going on strike demanding a fare hike, on which the government was not relenting. On 18 October 2000, talks between Murmu and private bus owners failed for the umpteenth time. The bus owners decided to stop running buses from the midnight of 20 October. The spokesman of the association Debasis Nayak told the press in Bhubaneswar that about 4,500 buses would be kept off the roads till their demands were met by the state government.[11] The final round of discussion between the technical committee of the government headed by the transport secretary in-charge, (late) Arun Kumar Samantaray, and the association failed.

On 21 October 2000, the All Orissa Bus Owners' Association withdrew its proposed strike after the state government, following Murmu's suggestion, effected a

---

[10] 'CM for Pro-Poor Transport Policy,' *The New Indian Express*, 19 June 2000.
[11] 'Talk Fails, Bus Owners to Make Good Strike Threat,' *The New Indian Express*, 19 October 2000.

3 paise/km hike in bus fare across the board. The town bus fare was also hiked by 50 paise. The decision was taken at a meeting that CM Patnaik had with the representatives of bus owners.

A PEOPLE'S PERSON

On the social side, Murmu loved to participate in events and gatherings even while being the minister. Be it birthdays, weddings, club functions, plantation drives or even typical tribal cockfights—a simple invitation would suffice to draw her to places. Most of her friends and acquaintances have mentioned some occasion or the other when Murmu visited them with gifts and spent time as a family member.

A perfectionist to the core, Murmu was never criticized for her work. She was known among her colleagues as a punctual leader for her resolve to reach every meeting ahead of schedule. In every village she visited, the villagers welcomed her with open arms. Probably Murmu was among the very few politicians who allowed people to meet her as and when they wished. At one point in time, apart from social work that she loved to do, she had said that in the life of a politician she led, she certainly missed her own relatives, who did not get much of her time when they needed her. 'But that was because once elected, I become people's leader, not just the family's. I also feel at times that I could have given some more time to my children and their studies, but there was nothing I could do once I got into the ministry full time,' she stated in an interview.[12] But she has also said

---

[12]'Tejasvani: Guest Draupadi Murmu, Governor of Jharkhand,' YouTube, http://bit.ly/3JJZBis. Accessed on 16 March 2023.

she feels happy that her children never raised any objections or expressed reluctance in any way. She has been vocal about the support she received from her husband. He was involved in her political career to a large extent, and that is why there were instances when people wanted to meet him and get their work done if they failed to reach the minister.

Murmu was accommodating and adjusting irrespective of the situation she was in. When her in-laws objected to her working in Bhubaneswar, she left her job without a single argument. She also got back to work and entered politics after her husband encouraged her to do so.

As someone who does not have a single blot on her career ever since she stepped into public life, Murmu is certainly an exception. Sources close to the family say that there were many people who wanted to seek favours from her by offering lakhs and crores of rupees even through her family members when she was the transport minister.[13] But her family members were averse to such deals. And Murmu, being a staunch disciplinarian, never acceded to such nefarious deals. She never allowed any kind of corrupt practices to touch her department officials, family members or the supporters who have stood by her.

However, she always paid heed to her close confidants when they requested her to help someone in dire need. Satish Samal reminisced:

> Some people kept approaching the minister for grants for one reason or another, and she used to send those people to me so that I could make a list of them and present it to her. I would take the liberty of picking

---

[13] As per Nabin Kumar Ram's interview with the author on 28–29 December 2022.

some names from the list and request her to grant a few thousand rupees to people who needed it for medical emergencies or other urgent issues. Jokingly, she would retort, 'So you have become the minister to decide who will get what!'

Even someone as close to Murmu as Ram corroborates that she never let her MLA local area development fund go to waste. 'She ensured that all of it was used for people. I remember Didi would make sure to use some amount of the funds everyday on some project or organization. She has done it throughout her tenure and I am sure she is among the very few of the legislators who have fully utilized the funds annually,' he said.

As a member of the home department's standing committee, she did not pay lip service only by producing reports based on others' perceptions. She used to visit all prisons in the state to see the condition of prisoners and know why they had been imprisoned for years. She used to speak to the prisoners who had been there for years without a single trial. Those visits shook her massively. She submitted a hard-hitting report to the government about the condition of the prisons and convicts who were languishing without anyone to stand up for them. She also suggested many corrective measures in the report that the government had to initiate to help reduce the inmates' detention in prisons for long by means of fast trials.[14]

Murmu was assigned government quarters in Unit 6, Bhubaneswar, where she would call her near and dear ones

---

[14] 'Emotional Speech by President Droupadi Murmu at Supreme Court Constitution Day Celebration,' YouTube, https://bit.ly/3n0vzhd. Accessed on 16 March 2023.

once in a while and spend time with them. Being a foodie, she cooked various dishes herself and served them to the people present there. As Delha Soren remembered, there have been many occasions when she and her family have visited Murmu in the quarters and eaten together. In those days, Murmu used to be a non-vegetarian and there was a flood of delicacies cooked and partaken by all. Soren remembered:

> But there were occasions when she did not have a house allotted in her name and she used to stay in the guest house or circuit house. On some days, she would just ring me up and say she was fed up eating guest house food. She would urge me to cook something typical to our community like saag for her. I would immediately cook and call her home. She has come to our house many times just to have a good meal.

ANANYA: MINISTERIAL INTEGRITY

Gandhian Aditya Patnaik, who left a life of luxury to run a free eye hospital in Rashgovindpur of Mayurbhanj district, tagged Murmu as a winner all the way given her struggles and achievements, both of which she has taken in her stride. She has been humble to a fault, never hankered for attention and has not elicited any complaints. 'She is "ananya" [unique],' said Patnaik. He recalled:

> When I launched the Mahatma Gandhi Eye Hospital and Research Institute here in Rashgovindpur and had invited the who's who, including then Vice President of India Krishan Kant, Naveen Babu had attended with his entire Cabinet. There were many other ministers,

including Murmu, but as per protocol, there were a limited number of seats on stage. So Murmu had to be seated in the audience. But she had no reaction and took it sportingly, though I apologized for not being able to get her seated on stage.'[15]

Murmu has also been a silent worker all along. She never got into any fight or face-off even with her political adversaries because she would prefer remaining silent instead of reacting. 'So if someone makes silence her dharma and works towards a goal with single-minded focus, I believe that is the mark of a true leader,' Patnaik averred.

'When an Adivasi walks, it becomes dance, when an Adivasi speaks, it becomes a song, and Madam Murmu personified this,' he explained, citing a Mundari saying that goes, '*Sen gi susun, kazi gee durang, doori gi dumang*' [Walking is dance, speaking is song and the body is mandar (drum)]. This is the life philosophy of the Adivasis.[16] 'The most inspiring aspect of Madam Murmu's journey is her village Uparbeda, which made her strong in the face of challenging situations, and today we have one of the strongest personalities as the president,' Patnaik said.

Looking forward to seeing Murmu at a new height of her career, he said, 'I hope she sticks to her own identity and honesty, which are her forte. Despite being nominated by a party, I believe she will not compromise on principles.' He also added:

---

[15] All quotes by Aditya Patnaik are from an interview conducted by the author on 28 December 2022.
[16] Priyanka, 'Hul Revolt in the Adivasi Songs of Jharkhand,' *Forward Press*, 10 July 2021, http://bit.ly/3LEokGb. Accessed on 21 March 2023.

I feel she could have done far more on jal, jungle aur jameen issues of the indigenous community, but maybe she was under some pressure when she was the governor of Jharkhand. Now when she is the president, all I can wish for is implementation of the Provisions of the Panchayats (Extension to the Scheduled Areas) Act (PESA) in Odisha. She made it possible in Madhya Pradesh and she can do it for Odisha.

On 6 August 2002, CM Patnaik initiated a major reshuffle in the Cabinet. Many people were incorporated into it and some who had already been in the Cabinet were moved to other departments. Some even had to forego their position from their respective ministries. Thus, two years into heading the commerce and transport ministry, Murmu's portfolio changed to fisheries and animal resources development.

Murmu's commitment to and discipline for work was such that on 18 September 2002, when the entire Cabinet, including CM Patnaik, stayed away from office during the bandh against the privatization of the National Aluminium Company (NALCO), Murmu was the only minister from the BJP who attended office. This was at a time when the BJP had also opposed both the bandh and privatization of NALCO. The state secretariat was deserted, with many employees taking leave to avoid problems. But nothing could deter Murmu from attending office, be it a strike or any other event.

Though the general election was due in 2005, it was advanced by a year to 2004. As Prabhu Chawla, the editorial director of *The New Indian Express*, wrote in *India Today*, 'It was simulated bravado at its worst when the BJP went for early elections. India was shining in a slogan and one section of the party—deputy prime minister L.K. Advani and party President M. Venkaiah Naidu particularly— thought this was the time, the time to declare the immortality of the NDA in power.'[17]

Murmu once again contested from the Rairangpur constituency as the BJP candidate in 2004. The JMM's Ramchandra Murmu was her contender. Till the last round of counting, the two contenders were neck-to-neck. At one point in the last round, when Murmu was leading by 1,500 votes, she fell unconscious due to exhaustion. Days of electioneering had taken a toll on her health. However, she won by a narrow margin of forty-two votes. 'I was the first one to congratulate her. It is the people's mandate and they vote for development. If people chose her, it must be respected,' said Ramchandra Murmu after she was elected president.[18]

He spoke highly of Murmu's organizational and behavioural skills. Terming her as the most cordial person, he said that they shared a wonderful relationship. 'She is like an elder sister to me. Whenever I have asked her for some help for people in the constituency, she has always come forward. Even my friends who had approached her for some help with my reference were welcomed and heard. Their problems were also solved,' he remembered. Murmu's concern for the people and her fearless nature came to the fore in an incident from 2006. This showed that she was

---

[17]Chawla, Prabhu, 'Elections 2004: BJP Pays Heavy Price for Arrogance, Haste and Strategic Blunders,' *India Today*, 24 May 2004, https://bit.ly/3EpC57i. Accessed on 21 February 2023.
[18]'I Lost to Her in Elections by 42 Votes, if Didi becomes President, I Will Have No Regrets for Losing,' YouTube, https://bit.ly/3M0mboh. Accessed on 29 March 2023.

active directly on the ground rather than restricted to her desk. On 2 January, violence over displacement at Kalinga Nagar in Jajpur rocked the state. This was caused by one of CM Patnaik's important steps to bring in industrialization in the state—setting up of a Tata Steel plant in the area.

As the tribals got this information, around 500 of them from Chandia, Gobarghati and Champakoila villages, armed with tribal weapons, including bows and arrows, reached the site of the proposed plant, where ground-levelling work was underway. The police had already been deployed in the area as a flag march had been conducted previously. Upon reaching the site, the tribals started pelting stones at the police, who tried to disperse them with tear gas shells and rubber bullets. However, the tribals were unrelenting and reportedly used crude bombs and arrows. On the fateful day, a policeman was caught by the tribals and butchered in public. This caused the police to open fire at a mob of the tribals, who were protesting the rehabilitation packages handed out to them, indiscriminately. Fourteen tribals, including a woman, were killed on the spot, and the protesters took the bodies of four of the tribals who had been killed with them. They were so irked that they laid siege to the Daitari–Paradip Express Highway. Immediately, fifteen platoons of Orissa State Armed Police were dispatched. A curfew was imposed.[19]

Chief Minister Patnaik was quick to declare an ex gratia of ₹1 lakh to the kin of each tribal who lost their life and said that the state government would bear the cost of treatment of the injured.

---

[19] 'Tribals Offer Tributes to Kalinga Nagar Victims,' *The New Indian Express*, 3 January 2023, http://bit.ly/3YSfSG8. Accessed on 16 March 2023.

With her tribal roots, it was a testing time for Murmu. She was not in the ministry but a legislator and, more importantly, a tribal leader from the BJP and the then state president of the BJP's Scheduled Tribe Morcha. She wanted to meet the tribals, and she did after the situation calmed.

According to Morada MLA Rajkishore Das, she visited the Kalinga Nagar site and discussed issues with the tribals. 'She probably wanted to stop the situation from escalating further,' said Das. Even though she was associated with the BJD–BJP alliance, her primary concern at that moment was the tribals. Hence, she decided to visit Kalinga Nagar without even thinking of the ramifications her visit could have. 'I came to know that she visited the spot as a government representative as well as an Adivasi. She was heard to have met the protesters not as a leader but as one among them and convinced them that the situation would improve,' said Das.

Apart from her work at the ground level, Murmu was also an able administrator. She was among the very few legislators to have never missed the House in session. During the Odisha Legislative Assembly sessions, Murmu was a regular attendee and participated in most of the discussions. She also made sure that any questions directed at her department were answered satisfactorily.

'The questions were carefully studied and answers were prepared with sufficient data and statistics. But Madam would rewrite her answers with the inputs and present it in the House,' remembered Samal. She used to participate in all demand discussions, zero hours and question hours. Murmu mentioned:

The questions I received were related to the functioning of my department or my area, so I never failed to participate. When questions were given to us eleven days in advance of the assembly session, I would write the answers based on thorough facts, records and data. I spent nights preparing the answers to questions without any help. There were jury members in the Assembly who notice members' participation and attendance. The jury members were from all parties, like the Congress, JMM and BJD, and they must have found my contribution worth appreciation.[20]

She was adjudged the best legislator for the year 2007 by the Odisha government and scripted history as the first woman and Adivasi to receive the Pandit Nilakantha Award. The awards for three consecutive years were announced only on 14 February 2009; Murmu won in the senior category for the year 2007.

Being in the ministry did not deter her from supporting the constituents on issues she felt strongly about. For instance, in 2007, she supported the people's demand to declare Rairangpur a separate district from Mayurbhanj. 'There are twenty-six blocks and a population of 22 lakh. The district administration cannot reach all of these blocks or people for welfare activities. Therefore, the demand for a new Rairangpur district is justified. It will bring back the regional imbalance on track. It is time the government agrees to the demand of district reorganization,' she stated while leading a protest rally on 27 December 2007. She

---

[20] 'An Exclusive Interview with India's First Tribal President, Draupadi Murmu by Dr Itirani Samanta,' YouTube, http://bit.ly/420iZ1w. Accessed on 10 March 2023.

insisted that this would usher in infrastructure development and revenue generation. But the demand remains unfulfilled even till date.

As a minister, she has been pretty successful, and her performance was highly appreciated. 'Her concepts are clear; she is firm, sharp and open. She is one of the very few persons to attend office every day. She was a regular at the party office even during her ministerial term at the grievance meetings. These things make her one of her kind,' said Surama Padhy describing Murmu.

Padhy lost the election in 2000 but regained the seat in 2004, while Murmu won both the elections. Murmu had the ministerial seat between 2000 and 2004 that, thereafter, went to Padhy. 'She had massive experience of the ministry and command over her department. She was never seen angry or upset with any officials. She often opted for open discussions—anyone in the department can discuss any subject with her,' remarked Padhy.

She looked up to Murmu as a first-time minister, so she wanted to meet Murmu and seek her guidance when she was given the responsibility of the ministry.

> But I was wary that because the ministry was given to me after 2004, she might be upset and angry with me. I mustered the courage one day to meet her and I was surprised by the way she hugged me. She said she was happy that I have got the ministry and she would always be there to work with me together for the betterment of people. This is only possible for Droupadi didi.

There were many times when Murmu discussed her constituency's problems with Padhy, and they would be sorted. 'We had an amicable relationship, rather friendly. When she had the seat, I used to go to her for my constituency's issues too,' said Padhy, adding that the best quality of Murmu is that she is a good listener.

Murmu was thorough in her work and listened to people, colleagues and other MLAs in the Assembly. She would then present the whole issue with such clarity and precision of thought that kept Padhy wondering as to how and where she got the courage to speak so well and lucidly. Her presentations were concise and to the point—something that everyone could understand, said Padhy, adding, 'I wish I could have learnt all that at the beginning of my political career. I was not as good a speaker as her.'

THE ALLIANCE COLLAPSES

The alliance between the BJD and the BJP came to an end in 2008, when Swami Lakshmanananda Saraswati was killed in Kandhamal on 23 August.

The then socio-economic condition of the tribals was not very good, and most areas lacked basic amenities and livelihood opportunities. These tribal-dominated pockets became a breeding ground for antisocial elements, including the Naxals. One of the most affected districts was Kandhamal, situated 255 km from Bhubaneswar.

The tribals from the interior pockets often fell prey to large-scale conversions to Christianity taking place then. It is believed that Christian missionaries were doing a lot of work in all the states of the country, and Odisha was no exception. Allegations of forced conversions of the tribals in lieu of money by the missionaries were at the forefront.

Lakshmanananda Saraswati dedicated his life to working for the tribals. He went to the Himalayas and became a *sanyasi* (hermit) but returned to Kandhamal. He vowed to fight the conversions, and for that purpose, set up an ashram at Chakapada for the tribal people. He established a school and *kanyashram* for the tribals. He was considered a preacher of Hindu spiritualism.

Lakshmanananda Saraswati had close ties with the RSS and was also against cow slaughter. He was vocal against Christian conversions and this was not liked by the missionaries.

It was for these reasons that Christian missionaries were blamed for the killing of the Swami. However, Maoist leader Sabyasachi Panda claimed responsibility for the murder at a time when rumours were rife that the missionaries had joined hands with the Maoists.

In fact, history is replete with reports of Panda's threats to kill L.K. Advani, Ashok Singhal and Praveen Togadia. Media reports stated that on the day of the Swami's death, the 130 girls, who were studying in the kanyashram of Tumudibandh in the district, witnessed the massacre, as they had come to the ashram for Janmashtami.[21]

The year was infamous in Odisha's history as the year of Maoists because twenty-eight commandos of the Special Security Force 'Grey Hounds' were ambushed by them. In another incident, seventeen police personnel were killed in a landmine explosion. The then MP Sudam Marndi was also attacked while three of his security personnel were killed.

But the killing of the Swami led to violent protests in many places, which led to sparks flying between the BJD

---

[21]Singh, Anupam Kumar, 'Bollywood Film for the Missionary Who Converted Hindus, Padma Shri to His Widow; Not Even a Discussion on the Saint Who Promoted Gharwapsi and Saved Cows,' *OpIndia*, 23 August 2022, https://bit.ly/3YPXr5K. Accessed on 21 February 2023.

and BJP, since the later was tagged as an outfit for Hindus with strong affiliation to the RSS and the Vishva Hindu Parishad.

On 7 March 2009, the BJD decided to part ways with the BJP. After two rounds of meeting with the BJP's Rajya Sabha MP Chandan Mitra, the BJD chief and Odisha CM Naveen Patnaik announced that the talks for the simultaneous Lok Sabha and Assembly elections in April 2009 had failed. 'The BJD and the BJP will go to the polls separately,' CM Patnaik stated.[22]

Murmu was asked by the party to contest for the Lok Sabha seat from Mayurbhanj and started staying at the headquarters of Baripada town for electioneering.

It is noteworthy that in the run up to the Lok Sabha elections, the BJD, Congress and even the JMM tried their best to woo Murmu to join them and contest the elections. Ram recollected:

> None dared to speak to Didi; it was Shyam Charan ji who used to be approached by the parties and lot of money was also offered. But Didi was principled, and so ingrained was her BJP ideology, she did not entertain any discussions on the matter. She would often say, 'I will never leave my party that has given me all that I am today.'

As campaigning started in earnest, Murmu relentlessly moved around Baripada town and visited every village, ward and house across the district. And this must have been a different election altogether for her, as it was for the Lok Sabha and included a larger base of people, both tribals

---

[22] 'BJD Severs Ties with BJP in Orissa,' *India Today*, 7 May 2009, http://bit.ly/40u4odt. Accessed on 16 March 2023.

and non-tribals. With most of her political career until then devoted to Rairangpur town and its periphery, she knew this was not going to be cakewalk for her.

Murmu had been a grassroots worker, but beyond Rairangpur, she did not have as much clout. She certainly made all the effort and the party too did not leave anything to chance to gain public trust. But it was a tough battle. In 2004, the BJD's Sudam Marndi was the incumbent while in 2009, the ruling BJD's Laxman Tudu was pitted against Murmu.

With the Kandhamal violence fresh in the minds of people, it had a cascading effect on all districts, including that of Mayurbhanj. Murmu attended many electioneering meetings despite instances of Maoist violence being reported every other day.

The Similipal Tiger Reserve area was the worst affected, with a series of mishaps being witnessed in quick succession. There were eighteen booths in Similipal, and the number of voters then stood at 11,021. The situation had turned very hostile and the government was under a lot of pressure to conduct polls in a peaceful manner. The impact of the violence being faced by the people in the area was so ghastly that not one official of the government wanted to be posted there. Human casualties and livelihood concerns were rife. Even the hospitals had neither doctors nor patients for days on end. In such a situation, Murmu did not hesitate to go out on her election campaigns. On one such campaigning day, 14 April 2009, Murmu toured many villages and addressed public gatherings in villages like Gurugudia extensively, where people feared to venture out.

She blamed the government for attributing the violence unnecessarily to the Maoists, even when most people knew it was the BJD's plan to garner votes by blaming the BJP. Murmu, in her address to a gathering in one of the villages, said:

> Every person in these villages is our own and I do not foresee any reason for fear. I do not agree that the posters found in these villages are any threat because I am sure it is the government which is making this in the name of Maoists so that none of the party members visit the village and they win the elections by way of power and money.

Until her visits, the villagers had been unhappy about no leader meeting them in their villages even as voting was only a few days away for the elections. Residents complained that the government had not done anything to contain the violence. Murmu's daring visits were able to change this perception. But it did not translate into votes for the BJP.

The 2009 elections were conducted, albeit with a security blanket in the villages and across the state. But Murmu lost the elections for the first time. She got 150,827 votes and placed third, while her rival from the BJD, Laxman Tudu, got 256,648 votes. In the second position was the JMM's Sudam Marndi, who got 190,470 votes.[23]

As the party pondered on the reasons for their failure and analysed the possible ways to bounce back the next time, Murmu got back to her life prior to contesting elections. She started to visit the villages and interact with people again. 'Even after losing elections, she has stayed

---

[23]'Mayurbhanj ST Election Results,' *Elections.in*, 10 June 2019, http://bit.ly/3FqIVtu. Accessed on 16 March 2023.

a non-controversial leader of the masses. Neither has she shown her anger or unhappiness nor did her losing election affect her life,' said Chotulal Mohanta.

Murmu also contested the 2014 Assembly Elections from her old seat, Rairangpur, but lost to the BJD's Saiba Sushil Kumar Hansdah. While Hansdah got 51,062 votes, Murmu managed 44,679 votes. Navjot Singh Sidhu, the cricketer–politician then in the BJP, went to Rairangpur in a chartered chopper to campaign for Murmu that year.

Naba Charan Majhi, the present MLA from Rairangpur, said:

> I was keen on fighting the election but the party decided to field her again and I had no reservations as Didi was a candidate from our party and for us our *sangathan* [party] matters the most. I never had nursed any animosity for this; rather, it strengthened my support to her and I was with her when she got the news to be the governor or even the President.[24]

THE BATTLE FOR A SANTALI SCRIPT

This phase of Murmu's career was also marked by an important, historic moment. She played a big role in getting the Santali language included in the Eighth Schedule of the Constitution in 2003, when the Atal Bihari Vajpayee government was in power at the Centre.

Santali, Murmu's mother tongue, is one of Austro-Asiatic sub-group of the Austric language group spoken mostly in Vietnam and Cambodia. It is spoken by 7.6 million people

---

[24] All quotes by Naba Charan Majhi are from an interview conducted by the author on 14 January 2023.

Droupadi Murmu (centre) as a student, with her classmates Dangi Murmu (left) and Sumitra Kisku (right), at Government Girls High School, Unit 2, in Bhubaneswar, Odisha.

Courtesy: Rashtrapati Bhavan

Murmu (fourth from left) with the staff and principal of Sri Aurobindo Integral Education and Research Centre, Rairangpur, Odisha, when she was a teacher in the school in 1994.

Courtesy: Rabindra Patnaik

With her students at Sri Aurobindo Integral Education and Research Centre, Rairangpur, in 1995.

Courtesy: Rabindra Patnaik

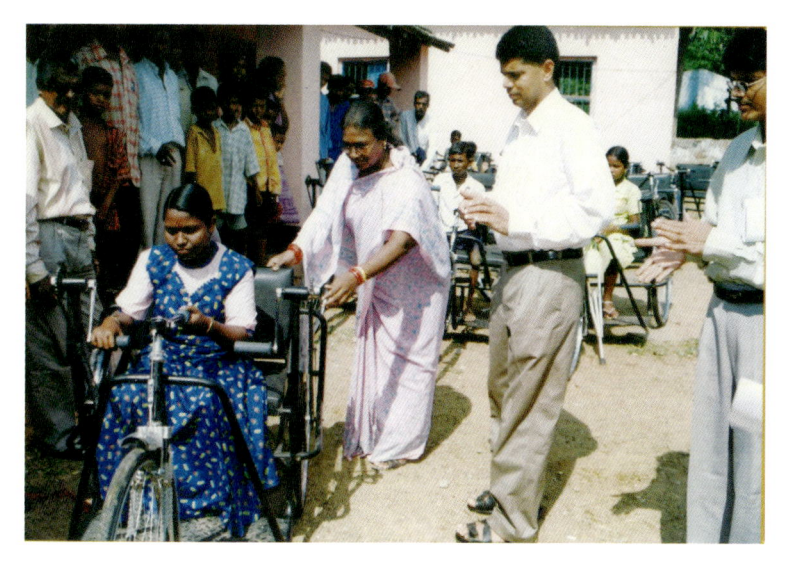

Murmu distributing tricycles at a camp for the specially abled between 2005 and 2007 as Member of Legislative Assembly (MLA). Also seen is the current 5T Secretary, Government of Odisha, V.K. Pandian, who was then the Mayurbhanj collector.

Courtesy: Nabin Kumar Ram

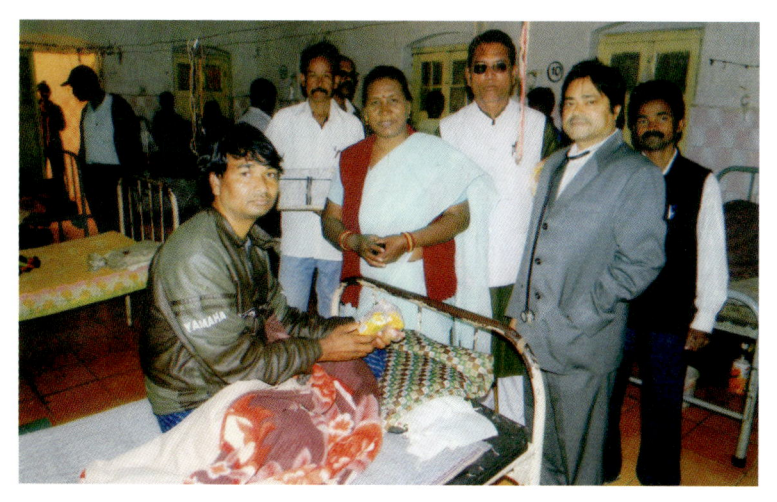

Murmu distributing bread to patients and attendants at a hospital in Rairangpur on Vajpayee Jayanti as the president of the Bharatiya Janata Party (BJP), Mayurbhanj west, in 2008.

Courtesy: Nabin Kumar Ram

Murmu cleaning the floor of a hospital during a cleanliness drive in Rairangpur when she was the president of the BJP, Mayurbhanj west, in 2009.

Courtesy: Nabin Kumar Ram

Murmu with daughter Itishree and son-in-law Ganesh Hembram (second from left) just before leaving for Ranchi to take over as the governor in May 2015.

Courtesy: Odisha TV

With Delha Soren (on her left), Murmu's roommate and companion during her stint in the irrigation department in the Government of Odisha, when Murmu was chosen as the governor of Jharkhand in May 2015.

Courtesy: Delha Soren

Murmu being administered the oath of office as governor of Jharkhand at Ranchi by Chief Justice Virendra Singh of the Jharkhand High Court on 18 May 2015.

Courtesy: Odisha TV

Murmu, during her gubernatorial term, offering prayers at Jagannath temple in Rairangpur in 2016.

Courtesy: Nabin Kumar Ram

Murmu participating in Rath Yatra at Rairangpur when she was the Rath Committee chairperson in 2016.

Courtesy: Nabin Kumar Ram

With school and college friend Chinmayee Gochchayat at Raj Bhavan in Ranchi when Murmu was the governor.

Courtesy: Chinmayee Gochchayat

Rabindra Patnaik, president of the school management committee of Sri Aurobindo Integral Education and Research Centre, Rairangpur, and his wife, Banajosna, congratulate Murmu on her nomination at Rairangpur in June 2022.

Courtesy: Rabindra Patnaik

With school friend Dangi Murmu at Mahanadi Coalfields Limited Guest House in Bhubaneswar before Murmu left for Delhi to file her nomination in June 2022.

Courtesy: Dangi Murmu

Murmu at a luncheon hosted by Odisha Chief Minister Naveen Patnaik (top left) at his residence Naveen Niwas in July 2022, when she reached Odisha to campaign ahead of the presidential election. Also seen are Gajendra Singh Shekhawat (bottom right) and Member of Parliament (MP) Pinaki Mishra (top right).

Courtesy: Information and Public Relations Department, Govt of Odisha

The Chief Justice of India, Justice N.V. Ramana, administering the oath of office of the President of India to Droupadi Murmu at her swearing-in ceremony in the central hall of Parliament, New Delhi, on 25 July 2022.

Courtesy: Rashtrapati Bhavan

Prime Minister Narendra Modi calling on President Murmu at Rashtrapati Bhavan for the first time on 26 July 2022 after her assumption of office.

Courtesy: Rashtrapati Bhavan

President Murmu pays homage to the brave soldiers who made the supreme sacrifice in the line of duty during the 1971 Bangladesh Liberation War at Albert Ekka War Memorial in Agartala in October 2022.

Courtesy: Rashtrapati Bhavan

President Murmu spinning the charkha during her visit to Sabarmati Ashram, Gujarat, in October 2022.

Courtesy: Rashtrapati Bhavan

President Murmu partaking mahaprasad with Puri's king, Gajapati Dibyasingha Deb, in November 2022.

Courtesy: Information and Public Relations Department, Govt of Odisha

President Murmu with her school friends at her alma mater Government Girls High School, Unit 2, Bhubaneswar, in November 2022.

Courtesy: Information and Public Relations Department, Govt of Odisha

President Murmu receives New Year greetings from students of various schools at Rashtrapati Bhavan.

Courtesy: Rashtrapati Bhavan

President Murmu graces the opening of the Amrit Udyan at Rashtrapati Bhavan in January 2023.

Courtesy: Rashtrapati Bhavan

With senior BJP leader from Mayurbhanj district, Nabin Kumar Ram, in February 2023 at Rashtrapati Bhavan.

Courtesy: Nabin Kumar Ram

in India. However, Santali never had a script, as there were no letters or alphabets for Santali phonemes, especially stop consonants and vowels. It was only an oral language for a very long time.

However, Pandit Raghunath Murmu became the first scholar to invent a script for Santali called 'Ol Chiki' in 1925. 'Ol' means writing and 'Chiki' means learning. The script was first put to use in a book *Hor Sereng* published in 1936 in Mayurbhanj, a district dominated by a tribal population.

Some scholars say that the need for a script was felt only after the missionaries started visiting the Santal-dominated areas in Jharkhand, Odisha and Bengal in the nineteenth century, as they needed to learn the language to better communicate with people.

Pandit Murmu, who passed away in 1982, used to say that the founder of the Norwegian Santal Mission, Lars Olsen Skrefsrud, wanted to introduce Santali language in schools to facilitate learning among tribal students.[25] Olsen Skrefsrud chose to write books in the Roman script that were used by students. This was the inspiration for Pandit Murmu to come up with a distinct script.

During those days (1908–09), while Pandit Murmu was in primary school, he wondered why he was not being imparted education in his mother tongue, Santali, but in Odia. He would ask his father to get him admitted to a school where Santali was the medium of education. But his father explained that Santalis did not have a script—it was only a spoken language. When he went to attend higher classes in another school, he would often scribble alphabets

---

[25]Pal, Suvam, 'Droupadi Murmu Rise Brings Back Tussle between Santali Scholars and Ol Chiki Govt Lobby,' *The Print*, 8 July 2022, https://bit.ly/3IU8Tql. Accessed on 6 March 2023.

and draw patterns on the playground, which is when he is believed to have started creating the Santali script. It was finally completed in 1925.[26]

According to Murmu, Pandit Murmu had been trying to spread and propagate the language in the Santal-dominated states, including Odisha, Jharkhand and West Bengal. He also appealed to the respective governments, both state and central, to accord it the status of a language, but nothing happened. There were many revolts and protests demanding the status of a language for Santali. But no headway was made.

Murmu felt that a tribe can survive only if it has its language, culture and tradition.[27] She met CM Patnaik at regular intervals in 2003, when she was a Cabinet member and an MLA, to have him accept the request for Santali to be accorded the status of a language so that a proposal could be sent to the Union government.

The Tribal Advisory Council, with tribal members including MLAs, used to be a nodal authority that functioned under the chairmanship of the CM. It was during her ministerial tenure that the council approved Murmu's request and forwarded it to the home department of the central government. Retired Chief Justice of India Ranganath Misra was then the chairman of the National Commission for Religious and Linguistic Minorities, also called Ranganath Misra Commission. It was constituted

---

[26]Hembrom, Anubha, 'Why Guru Gomke Pandit Raghunath Murmu Created The Santali Script?,' *Adivasi Lives Matter*, 5 May 2022, https://bit.ly/3JTV3pw. Accessed on 21 March 2023.
[27]'An Exclusive Interview with India's First Tribal President, Draupadi Murmu by Dr. Itirani Samanta,' YouTube, http://bit.ly/420iZ1w. Accessed on 10 March 2023.

by the Government of India on 29 October 2004 to look into various issues related to the linguistic and religious minorities of India. He was the one who appreciated the proposal. 'To gain the status [of a language], the script needed acceptance by the concerned department. Member of the thirteenth and fourteenth Lok Sabha Kharabela Swain from the BJP encouraged me and we decided to meet PM Vajpayee ji. He was happy and immediately gave us assurance to accord it the status of language,' Murmu recollected.[28]

The Eighth Schedule to the Constitution consists of twenty-two languages: Assamese, Bengali, Gujarati, Hindi, Kannada, Kashmiri, Konkani, Malayalam, Manipuri, Marathi, Nepali, Odia, Punjabi, Sanskrit, Sindhi, Tamil, Telugu, Urdu, Bodo, Santali, Maithili and Dogri. Of these, Bodo, Dogri, Maithili and Santali were added in 2004. At present, there are demands of thirty-eight more languages to be included in the Eighth Schedule.

Murmu fondly remembered how the CM of Odisha appreciated her efforts and thanked her on the floor of the Assembly. She felt gratified and also thanked the CM for sending the proposal at the right time.

Swain said that it was easy for him to get associated with the Ol Chiki movement of the Santalis even though he is a non-Adivasi. He lent support to the movement of getting Santali included in the Eighth Schedule of the Constitution when the JMM raised the issue in early 2000, but the movement did not gather momentum until Murmu took up the cause and led the demand for its inclusion. He stated:

---

[28]Ibid.

When I got to know about Droupadi Murmu raising pitch for the demand, I wanted to be with her in the movement. She is an Odia, an Adivasi and a Santali. To top it all, she is our sister. I must be with her. So when she called me up one day to say that she wants to take the cause to the PM, I was in Delhi and asked her to reach the capital as soon as possible.[29]

The day Murmu reached the PMO with the state government approval on the script, Swain accompanied her. 'I have this uncanny habit of getting my appointments in moments with the BJP top brass. The moment we reached Vajpayee ji's chamber, we got an entry for the meeting. Vajpayee ji and Murmu ji spoke for about forty-five minutes and discussed the possibility of Ol Chiki being included in the Schedule and the rest is history,' he said with a smile.

He remembered that within a few days, the script was included in the Schedule, and Murmu helmed a massive function at Chhau Padia, a field in Rairangpur, to celebrate the victory. Thousands of Adivasis congregated there, and he was invited as a special guest. Swain was also made to sit on the dais, even if the others on the stage were Adivasis. 'I delivered a speech in Odia and was felicitated on the stage by Murmu, who appreciated my effort to take the issue forward,' Swain fondly remembered.

'She is uncomplicated and honest, that's what touches me the most about her,' Swain remarked on Murmu as a person.

Santali experts and academics feel that Murmu's

---

[29] All quotes by Kharabela Swain are from an interview conducted by the author on 10 January 2023.

The One with No Peer: On-Ground Legislation 135

Santali identity and her elevation to India's highest constitutional office could bring both her community as well as language to the national spotlight.[30]

Many Santali books have been published since then in the Ol Chiki script. Besides, Santali magazines in Ol Chiki are also being published regularly. The University Grants Commission (UGC) introduced Santali as a subject for the National Eligibility Test in 2013. On 7 December 2019, Sarojini Hembram, a BJD member nominated to the Rajya Sabha, addressed the House in the Santali language and was appreciated by the then Speaker Venkaiah Naidu.

On 29 May 2022, PM Modi, while addressing the eighty-ninth episode of *Mann Ki Baat*, appreciated Shripati Tudu's efforts in preparing a version of the country's Constitution in Ol Chiki for the Santali community.[31] Tudu is a professor of Santali language at Sidho-Kanho-Birsha University and started translating the 235-page document into the Santali script in 2019 with the objective of making it readable for lakhs of tribal people and creating awareness about their rights.

The battle to obtain the status of a language for her mother tongue was only one of the many issues that Murmu took up. Her work extended to various social and political issues, and these reflected in the progress of her political career as well. After being elected MLA in 2000, Murmu became the member of House Committee on Railway between 2000 and 2001, Committee on Welfare of

---

[30] Pal, Suvam, 'Droupadi Murmu Rise Brings Back Tussle between Santali Scholars and Ol Chiki Govt Lobby,' *The Print* 8 July 2022, https://bit.ly/3IU8Tql. Accessed on 6 March 2023.

[31] 'PM Narendra Modi's 89th Edition of Mann Ki Baat | 29th May 2022', YouTube, https://bit.ly/3YTLcUW. Accessed on 16 March 2023.

SC and ST between 2004 and 2005, House Committee on Women and Child Welfare between 2004 and 2005, House Committee on Protection of Forests between 2004 and 2005 and Subject Committee on Panchayati Raj between 2004 and 2005.

She was also the president of the Mayurbhanj district unit of BJP from 2002 to 2009, state president of the Scheduled Tribe Morcha of Odisha from 2006 to 2009 and president of the Mayurbhanj district unit of BJP in 2010 and from 2013 to 2015.

In 2013, Murmu was appointed as the national executive member of the Scheduled Tribe Morcha of the BJP—a post she held till 10 April 2015.

5

Warm Clothes in the Winter, an Umbrella in the Rain: Grief and Spirituality

In 2000, Murmu had called her mother and one of the brothers to stay with her at Rairangpur, as it was difficult for them to survive due to financial constraints. Since they were not educated, they could not take up any business either. As she had promised to stand by her family, Murmu wanted to do something for her brother and his family. Apart from buying them a piece of land nearby, she also rebuilt the old house at Uparbeda, where she had grown up.

Her brother and sister-in-law accompanied her to Bhubaneswar when she got into the ministry and continued to stay in the capital city for the most part. In fact, they used to take care of Murmu's family and children when she was busy with work. In 2009, as Murmu lost the Lok Sabha election from the Mayurbhanj Lok Sabha constituency, she decided to go back to Rairangpur to work with and for the people, while her elder son Laxman, then twenty-five years old, remained in Bhubaneswar with his maternal uncle, as some of his training was still pending.

TRAGEDY: THE TURN TO SPIRITUALITY

It was during Murmu's absence from Bhubaneswar on 26 October 2009 that she got a call from her brother about her son Laxman not waking up in the morning after returning late from a party with his friends.

The twenty-five-year-old was found in an unconscious state in his bed that morning. He was taken to a private hospital and was later shifted to Capital Hospital, where he was declared brought dead. The police said that Laxman had been with his friends for dinner and was brought back in an unstable condition. 'Presuming him to be sleepy, his uncle and aunt did not disturb him. However, he did not wake up in the morning and was found unconscious. When he was rushed to hospital, Laxman was dead. His body did not bear any external injury mark,' the *The New Indian Express* reported.[1]

However, the police suspected that Laxman might have fallen off the bike while returning home with his friend and could have had a fatal head injury, which led to his death.

Murmu rushed to Bhubaneswar with Ram and some of her family members. By the time she reached the capital, some of her close friends and acquaintances were already at the hospital. No one dared to call her at that time, but Delha Soren did so while Murmu was on the way to Bhubaneswar to enquire how far she had reached.

Soren recollected emotionally:

> Since I was the first one to speak to her, she blurted out what she was feeling. For the first time, I heard

---

[1] 'Ex-Minister's Son Dies Mysteriously,' *The New Indian Express*, 27 October 2009, https://bit.ly/3Ip2OlC. Accessed on 22 February 2023.

her cry. She asked me why I did not save her son, why I did not do anything to keep him alive, which was all an outburst of her pain and anguish. I consoled her as much as I could, but she was a mother. It is difficult to make a mother understand when she loses a child.

Soren remembers how difficult it was to console Murmu after she reached the hospital.

It was a trying time for all of us to see such a strong woman breaking down so badly. It was obvious for her to not believe that something like this could happen. She shook her son, asking him to wake up. She kept saying, 'You had training today, how can you not wake up and appear for the exams!' It took her a long time to come to terms with reality.

As the formalities had to be completed on time for the funeral rites, Ram, along with many other party supporters, arranged the required documentation. The party members had always been with her through the ups and downs of her life, and they were all there through this trying time as well, according to Ram. He said:

I do not think there was a minute other than the time she slept that I was not there with her. We did not want her to go into shock or depression, so we ensured we stayed close to her and kept her mind diverted. As soon as the last rites were over, we wanted to distract her so that she could get back to work, which could heal her emotionally too.

Since most of the time she remained quiet, consumed by grief and pain, many people offered her advice to adopt some spiritual methods that could help her balance her state of mind. Back then, she was not in a state to accept any advice. She did visit the nearby Brahma Kumari (BK) ashram but was not ready to absorb any advice from the BK sisters on how to deal with the crisis.

Over a short period of time, Murmu's visits to the BKs regularized. While she was listening to the teachings mechanically in the beginning, she soon started taking them seriously and became an ardent follower of the sect.

For days, she would enter the ashram and just sit there blankly for hours. Even when she attended a *pravachan* [preaching] by one of the sisters, she was not receptive at all, as if she was in a trance. After a few days, however, she started to register the messages that the BKs shared with her. By her own admission, during some media interviews, she mentioned what an important role the ashram played in bringing back her balance of mind. She said:

> At a time when I had lost the will to survive and had gone into depression, the BKs helped me come back to life. They infused in me the feeling of living a life that is worthwhile in many other ways. My life is not only for me, it has other people who look up to me. I had completely ignored that my daughter needed me, my brother and my party too needed me. Whatever is left in me must be devoted to all who have made me what I am today.[2]

She went into depression for at least two months. At a time when people thought she would not survive the pain, she made up her mind to fight her own fears and loss. '*Lekin*

---

[2] 'How Raj Yoga Changed the Course of Murmu's Life | DRAUPADI MURMU | Brahma Kumaris | Godlywood Studio |,' YouTube, http://bit.ly/3TuqjP4. Accessed on 21 March 2023.

jeene ke liye ek aadhar chahiye [There has to be some reason to live],' she said.³ That was when she called up the BKs.

Murmu learnt Raj Yoga in 2009 and used to visit the BK ashram in Rairangpur many times, but she could not concentrate. However, over time, she became an integral part of the sisters' visits to various remote villages to spread the teachings of Shiv Baba, the human incarnation who was considered the *nirakar paramatma* [formless divine power], the *shaktibindu* [point of enlightenment]. His teachings define the spiritual fabric of the BKs.

Brahma Kumari Supriya from the ashram in Rairangpur reminisced:

> After being introduced to the BKs, she used to attend many of our functions like Shiv Ratri, Rakshabandhan and Jhanki as a guest. Later on, she had the opportunity to meet Dadi Janaki and Prakashmani, who blessed her to be at ease with herself. *Sthiramana* is not an easy way—it takes a while to surrender and become one with oneself. She learnt and healed. She did not know how to use the teachings in her life initially, but she learnt it over a period of time. A time came when she said that she had received God's message, which taught her many things.⁴

But destiny could not have been crueller, as she faced the deaths of her family members within a span of five years. Whenever she gathered courage to begin life anew, yet another disaster shook her, as if her patience was being tested by God. In hindsight, only Murmu, with her immense strength, could have withstood the tests she faced.

---

³Ibid.
⁴All quotes by BK Supriya are from an interview conducted by the author on 27 December 2022.

FROM GRIEF TO SPIRITUALITY

In 2013, Murmu lost her younger son Sipun to an accident. Sources close to her family said that she was overprotective of him. After a health condition damaged his eyesight, she would not allow him to travel after dark. That fateful night, after Murmu left home for a social function, her son, without paying any heed to his mother's advice, started out on his bike. That was when he reportedly met with an accident and passed away on the spot. While some people from Rairangpur who know her believe this tragic accident to be the result of some political animosity, others say it was an accident that turned fatal.

The Murmu couple was inconsolable in Rairangpur, losing their second son even before they could recover from the trauma of the death of their eldest son. Once again in the throes of grief, Murmu looked inwards and stopped meeting people or even going out. Further tragedy befell the family when Murmu's daughter-in-law, Sipun's pregnant wife, had a miscarriage and left for her paternal home. That added to Murmu's pain, leaving her with emotional scars. Soren said that Murmu would console herself by saying that Sipun's child would give them much-needed solace, but that too did not happen.

The BKs visited her to bring her into their fold for relief. She patiently heard them but did not respond at that time. 'She seemed brave enough even when she had lost the second child. She was one of those who dipped in grief without showing it to the world. We offered her to visit us and practise meditation, but nothing seemed to register in her mind,' said BK Supriya.

Murmu was in for more trouble when Shyam Charan

started falling ill. He went into depression and was in and out of hospitals frequently. He was admitted to Kalinga Hospital in Bhubaneswar, which was then one of the premier healthcare institutions of Odisha. After undergoing treatment for liver cirrhosis for months, he wanted to go back to Rairangpur.

Murmu was not doing any better. Along with the crises in her family, she was also facing challenges on the political front. Her connect with people, which could have made her feel better, was also waning due to her inability to cope with so many losses. She was completely broken and found it impossible to get back to normal life.

It was on 1 August 2014 that she lost her husband Shyam Charan. Between 2009 and 2014, Murmu also lost her mother and one of her brothers too. It was hard to imagine that Murmu would ever bounce back from her losses, though every effort was made by the party functionaries to keep her spirited with some event or the other.

In spite of so much pain, she has remained firm. When she was going through the toughest time of her life, Surama Padhy and her husband met her many times. They had, over a period of time, become family friends. 'I salute her determination, strength and conviction in the face of a mountain of difficulty. Her feet never shook. She was ready to face it all. She is different. We would talk for hours at times and share our concerns,' Padhy said.

People who knew the Murmu couple say they were an ideal pair. Soren said that Shyam Charan was very close to her husband, and their families spent a lot of time together. 'I have never ever seen them having any discord. It was as if they were made for each other. I remember the support

Shyam Charan lent Droupadi during her entry into politics and her journey. He was also very cordial and soft-spoken, so both were happy until the deaths of their sons,' she reminisced.

Rabindra Patnaik, who was a colleague of Shyam Charan, had words of praise for him as well. He remembered:

> He was friendly and good humoured. He was the one who wanted Murmu to join some job because he cared a lot about her. He wanted her to go ahead in life as she was educated and being an Adivasi can do a lot of work for the tribe. I remember almost anyone who wanted to meet Murmu went through Shyam Charan because he was equally approachable. I used to go their house and they too came to us.

Padhy said that all the problems Murmu faced made her stronger. 'She has a steely resolve and continues to have control over all her actions. She was shaken with the losses, true, but she also gained control of her circumstances by getting ready to face life after every adverse situation,' she said.

The party members, including Prahallad Dora and then education minister Bimbadhar Nayak, who always used to be with her, had suggested talking to the BKs much earlier in 2002. 'But then I had no time to undertake a course or attend their classes,' Murmu had said.[5] After her second son's death, Murmu had called the BKs to her Rairangpur home. Later, the sect convinced her to visit the ashram for at least five to ten minutes, but that too seemed difficult

---

[5]'Draupadi Murmu Speech | Draupadi Murmu Addressing at Sonotel Garden | Brahma Kumaris Dhanbad | 2017,' YouTube, https://bit.ly/3LtmojH. Accessed on 16 March 2022.

to her. Even when she did go, she was absent-minded. Her second son's death had depressed her so much that she was only seen crying. Every moment tears would well up in her eyes and roll down her cheeks.[6]

Murmu reminisced in an interview about how, years ago, the BK sisters made her compare life with halwa and said, '*Halwa jab pak jaata hai to kadhai se* detach *ho jata hai*,' meaning that when one matures, one must be detached.[7] But nothing registered in her mind. 'How do I control my mind? I did yoga in the ashram to get strength,' Murmu said. She also got a spiritual calling from the BKs when she lost her first son. But she remained ignorant about it. She said that the will of God works only when He wishes to.

Brahma Kumari Supriya recollects how Murmu came out of her grief and depression through meditation and spiritual healing at the ashram. She was emotionally exhausted and not able to sustain any further mental trauma or grief. After her first son's death, she did not talk to anyone or eat properly for six months. Brahma Kumari Supriya added that later she went to the Mount Abu ashram of the BKs in Rajasthan, and surrendered to the will of God.

After regular spells of meditation and sessions of spiritual discourse, she seemed to attain peace

---

[6] "How Raj Yoga Changed the Course of Murmu's Life | DRAUPADI MURMU | Brahma Kumaris | Godlywood Studio |,' YouTube, http://bit.ly/3TuqjP4. Accessed on 21 March 2023; 'Draupadi Murmu Speech | Draupadi Murmu Addressing at Sonotel Garden | Brahma Kumaris Dhanbad | 2017,' YouTube, https://bit.ly/3LtmojH. Accessed on 16 March 2022.

[7] "How Raj Yoga Changed the Course of Murmu's Life | DRAUPADI MURMU | Brahma Kumaris | Godlywood Studio |,' YouTube, http://bit.ly/3TuqjP4. Accessed on 21 March 2023.

and tranquility. These things helped her overcome grave personal tragedies in her life. Murmu also has acknowledged how the teachings and meditation technique of the BKs helped her relive life.[8] Murmu has given away a part of her ancestral home to the BKs so that they can start courses in the village. She also plans to give away her Rairangpur home to the sect.

Brahma Kumari Supriya explained:

> *Halchal ke andar achal raho* [Stay firm even in the midst of unrest] was a message that worked for Arjuna in our myths and we asked her to follow that. We would give her our best of comfort through our guiding principles. We noticed that she started changing, though the healing process was delayed. We took her to *Geeta Pathshala* (school for teaching the Geeta) and made her participate in *Ishwariyasandesh*—message from God. We moved around villages with campaigns against alcoholism and other issues to uplift the life and society and she would be a part of it.

Family members corroborate that once she accepted the BK way of life, she changed her lifestyle, including her food habits. She would wake up by 3.00 a.m. every day at *Brahmamuhurta* [time of the creator] and meditate for hours. She would walk for 5 km and come back to start life afresh. Even when she was delayed because of any function or party work till late at night, she would still get up at 3.00 a.m. She only had *sattwik* food, which meant her meals were vegetarian, without onion and garlic. For more than ten years, she has followed the same regime.

---

[8]Ibid.

Addressing a BK centre in Bokaro, Murmu stressed on the inherent power of women, which has the capacity to steer the world towards a better tomorrow. 'Women are instrumental in the development of the world but, for that, education is important. Once women are educated and treated equally, there will be solutions to all kinds of problems,' she said after inaugurating a Raj Yoga Bhavan of the BKs.[9]

The members of the sect feel that her commitment to spiritualism is unique. One who can commit to God, the Divine, the Supreme power, can commit to the cause of the people.

'*Gyana, yoga, dharana, seva* [knowledge, yoga, concentration and service] are the most important values and Droupadi is a combination of everything. She would first go to the meditation room and then come out to interact with us. She was involved in seva. Spiritually empowered, she achieved peace, calmness, happiness and also got rid of any negative feelings about life,' said BK Supriya.

In one of the meetings, Murmu had said that she did what Shiv Baba told her—the Almighty does not like crying faces. When a person leaves their body for eternal deliverance, their lives flash in front of them. 'I would not like to see a portrait of me crying. From that day, I decided not to cry ever again,' she said.[10] She went on to say that while teaching at the Sri Aurobindo Integral School,

---

[9]@rashtrapatibhvn, 'LIVE: President Droupadi Murmu Addresses the National Convention on "Women as Foundation of Value-Based Society" at Gurugram,' *Twitter*, https://bit.ly/42P8Hlz. Accessed on 16 March 2023.
[10]'Draupadi Murmu Speech | Draupadi Murmu Addressing at Sonotel Garden | Brahma Kumaris Dhanbad | 2017,' YouTube, https://bit.ly/3LtmojH. Accessed on 16 March 2022.

the principal of the school had told her that as we guide children or even scold them to put them in the right path, similarly, God decides to give us lessons of life in His own way to perhaps teach us something. 'God chooses His own children and I believe, God chose me,' she said.[11] Murmu added:

> Like warm clothes protect in winter, umbrella in rain and footwear in summer, God's blessings protect humans from storms. Humans have a lot of shakti and it is important to nourish that shakti within us. *Antarmukhibano* [see inward/within]. In human life, hardly 2–4 per cent shakti is used and rest goes to waste. So, to fully harness our Shakti, we need to be attached to God so that he guides us for our betterment and others' as well. *Biswakalyankaribano* [do good to the world]. But first empower yourself. Only when you have surplus can you give to others. To enjoy life, you must introspect and decide if you are doing right. I keep listening to Geeta Gyan from Behenji (BK Supriya). I keep attending BK meetings and other similar spiritual discourses as I am greedy for knowledge, for good vibration because I believe that good vibes can only infuse positivity into us.[12]

Despite facing hardships, Murmu stayed positive, perhaps because she believed that the world can be a better place if we live with positivity. Her trust in the supreme power, that is, God, kept her going through tough times. She said that poking a wound makes it septic and that is why she

---

[11] Ibid.
[12] Ibid.

avoids thinking about her pain. Having spent her childhood happily, she felt that her later life was very different and painful. Talking about the loss of her near and dear ones as life-shattering, she said that she lived only for her daughter and vice-versa. After facing many challenges, the BK ashram helped her deal with pain and struggle through meditation and service to people. Today, she is an example of a strong personality, who was able to turn her weakness into strength.[13]

Murmu has not only been associated with the BKs but also with many other sociocultural and religio-spiritual organizations since 2000.

After her association with the sect, as she started becoming her normal self, many BJP workers who had stood by her during the difficult days wanted her to get involved in party work once again. They would convince her to get into the regular schedule to bounce back into politics, but she was reluctant. She wanted to leave politics and get back to her family life. Her daughter, Itishree; her brother, Taranisen, and his wife were all that was left of her family. But the party was also her family.

'Since I and Naba bhai (Naba Charan Majhi, current MLA from the party for Rairangpur) were mostly with Didi, we convinced her to attend some party functions so that she could change her mind. We would refuel her car and drive her to various programmes,' said Ram.

They accompanied Murmu to Jharkhand when elections were in the offing. She stayed there for a few days. They also took her to the training camp in Puri, when Ramlal ji from the RSS was present so that she could

---
[13]Ibid.

interact with him. She also went to Indore and Delhi for various party programmes with Ram and Majhi. 'Our purpose was to involve Didi in party work so that she does not remain drowned in pain. She was very restricted in mingling with people for that stretch of time. We wanted her to come out of that quagmire and return to normalcy,' said Majhi.

These trips worked well for Murmu and helped her change her mind. She got involved in party work once again. As normalcy returned, Murmu wanted her daughter to get married. Itishree was initially reluctant, as she had seen her mother struggle in the past few years. But Murmu convinced her daughter. An employee of United Commercial (UCO) Bank by then, Itishree married rugby player Ganesh Hembram in 2015. He, too, works in a bank.

TOWARDS GOVERNORSHIP

In the meantime, Murmu received a call from the Centre in the early months of 2015 to submit some of her academic and work documents. Unaware of the reason, Murmu thought that the party could be trying to reinstate her in some corporation considering her past work. She was also shocked to learn that police verification about her was underway in Mayurbhanj. But she had no clue as to why all these documents were required and verification was being done.

In a few days, she got to know that she had been chosen to become the governor of Jharkhand. While the state of Jharkhand has a majority tribal population, it is also close to Mayurbhanj and Rairangpur, in particular, with a mountain range separating the two states.

It was also heard that since the BJP was in power then in Jharkhand, the party found Murmu to be the best candidate, as she was an educated tribal woman.

Murmu's personal assistant during her term as a governor, Bikash Chandra Mohanto, present legislator Majhi and senior party member Ram were together at a wedding party when the BJP's central leadership called her to break the news that she had been chosen to be the governor. Majhi recollected that hearing this, she burst into tears.

Murmu has been nurtured by the party, and workers like Majhi and Ram have always been by her side and respected her like an elder sister. 'When she got the call for governorship, all three of us were at an event, and when she got to know about her presidentship, I was 2 km away from her house in Rairangpur. I left everything and rushed to her residence when I saw the house crowded, with Didi at the centre of all attention,' Majhi recollected. 'We do not address party people as sirs and madams; we believe in the concept of Bhai and Didi. She calls us Bhai and we address her as Didi, and this relationship lasts beyond party affinity as well,' he added.

After being selected, on 12 May 2015, she addressed the townspeople and the people of the district at a public gathering:

> I am thankful to the government for giving me this opportunity to serve people. The legislative, executive and judiciary are three important wings of the government, and I will exercise powers to give my views and opinion. I will try to live up to the expectations of the people and the government. This is not only

a responsibility as the top-most position of a state but all over India, tribals and downtrodden are a deprived lot. I will try to take care of them and uplift them. I am grateful to the people of Rairangpur for the love they have given me over the years.

She reminded everyone that the government created the tribal development ministry and Jual Oram, a tribal, was heading it. She also thanked the government for keeping its word to take care of the health and education requirements of the downtrodden and the marginalized.

Before leaving Rairangpur to begin her tenure as the governor of Jharkhand on 12 May 2015, she became emotional.

I need your good wishes so that I can take care of Jharkhand's all round development. I will uphold the dignity of the post of the governor, for, it is not only a position but a responsibility. Not only in Jharkhand, but I will do things that will be for the betterment of all Adivasis, tribes and downtrodden people in the country. I will suggest changes to the government for uplifting of the marginalized people. It is now my time to repay the love I was given by everyone.

I want to win the trust of the people of Jharkhand in the same way as I did here in my homeland. I will do all that I can to be with people and take their voice to the government. The more the human resource is developed the more the state grows. I will lay emphasis on education as the first step.

The NDA government has always given importance to people from the backward sections of society. I thank the central government for the proactive steps they are taking to include the marginalized population in the mainstream.

'She is the daughter of the state and made us proud,' said Ram, remembering the day Murmu left her hometown for Ranchi.

Ranjan Patel, the BJP's senior leader and functionary in western Odisha, who was also in charge of the party in Jharkhand, was asked to reach Rairangpur immediately to accompany Murmu to Ranchi. He reminisced:

> I felt so happy that one of our party leaders has been selected as the governor. I rushed to Rairangpur. The field where the chopper was all set was filled with lots of supporters. People waited for hours to catch a glimpse of Murmu before she left for her new assignment. After I reached, Didi made salutations to all the people who had congregated and we rushed to board the chartered chopper. I accompanied her till Ranchi and wished her luck.

Murmu was sworn in as the governor of Jharkhand on 18 May 2015, becoming the first woman to hold the position. The BJP was in power in Jharkhand for most of her six-year tenure as a governor and was also in power in the Union government throughout her tenure.

TURNING GRIEF TO GOLD: THE SCHOOL

Before Murmu left for Ranchi, she began an important project. Having faced problems in getting educated due to the absence of higher education institutes in her native place, Murmu decided to give a good turn to the lives of tribal children who continue to be deprived of good schools. After her husband's demise, there was no one left to care for the landed property in her in-laws' village of Pahadpur. Murmu had been contemplating starting a school for the less privileged from the tribal pockets of the state. With a group of supporters, who were also active members of the BJP, she sat and discussed how to take her plan forward. After months of preparation and arrangement of infrastructure, she decided to open the school without further delay and wanted admissions to begin. She decided to start classes in Shyam Charan's existing house. The members discussed when finances could be arranged and renovation and construction be taken up, provided the student strength grew.

After her selection as governor, though she was away in Ranchi, people back home oversaw the construction and other requisites of the school. In 2016, the Shyam, Laxman, Sipun (SLS) Memorial Residential School, in memory of her husband and two sons, was finally opened for admissions on the 4.5 acre land in Pahadpur.

Around 5 km from Balbhadrapur, en route to Rairangpur from Jashipur Chhak, there are clear directions towards Murmu Square. From there, the pointers at every junction direct visitors to the school. After another 5 km, a bust of Shyam Charan Murmu just outside the school welcomes you. The premises have a large gate. Once you enter the gate, you see hostels for boys and girls on either side. A few steps forward take you to the classrooms for Classes 6 to 10. Exactly in the middle is a well-manicured garden space that is barricaded and has life-like busts of Shyam Charan, Laxman and Sipun. Keeping the memory of Murmu's near and dear ones alive, the statues remind everyone of how the challenges of her life have taken the shape of opportunities for less privileged children.

Presently, a total of eighty-one students are enrolled in the residential school. There are around ten full-time teachers and a headmaster besides a caretaker. The school is affiliated to the Board of Secondary Education, Government of Odisha. There are others to take care of the hostel affairs as well.

The classrooms are sparkling clean with tiled floors, tables and chairs, stationery, books and other requisite items. The Indian Oil Corporation, too, donated ₹68 lakh to the school in 2019 for its development.

Since the school is close to Murmu's heart and she has sculpted it step by step, people in Pahadpur say that she seems the happiest when she is on the campus. Prior to her term in Ranchi, she used to visit the place frequently to oversee the preparations and, after the school opened, she made it a point to go there at regular intervals. She personally monitored the facilities and ensured that the students got the best of education. She spent a fair amount of time with the students discussing their studies.

'The last time she visited the school was on 13 June 2022 when she spent the entire day with us. When here, she also eats with the children and interacts with them,' said Narayan Hansda, the hostel in-charge who also doubles as the clerk.[14]

There is an admission fee for the school for general candidates, but the SC and ST students can enrol and study for free. Every year, on her husband's death anniversary

---

[14]Quote from an interview conducted by the author on 13 November 2022

on 1 August, Murmu spends the day at the school. A puja is organized and special food is prepared for students and villagers. It is usually her associates and party members, like Ram or former Bank of India official Ishwar Mishra, who oversee the arrangements on the death anniversary of Shyam Charan in her absence.

However, in 2022, she had to be in New Delhi and could not attend the function. Whenever she had problems in attending the event, she would depute some responsible family or friends to arrange everything for the ritualistic observation of the day.

A student of the SLS Memorial School said:

> 'Fix your eyes and heart on the goal so much so that you do not have time to waste', she would say. She teaches us general knowledge and science, and interacts with us whenever she is here. Didi (as the students fondly refer to her) gives us life lessons and her life is so inspiring that when we hear the stories, we are inspired to do something good for our motherland.[15]

Even when she was the governor, she would sit with them and teach. That is something special that the children of the school remember with fondness.

Munna Pratihari, who has been the vice president of the SLS Memorial School since its establishment, lives on the school premises and looks after its management. Speaking of the selection criteria, he said that those students whose scores are below 30 per cent are usually given preference for admission in the school. That is the motto, he asserted.

---

[15]Quote from an interview conducted by the author on 12 November 2022

'We try to enhance the academic standard of the below-average students and bring them at par with other students. It is heartening that all the twenty students of the school in Class 10 secured first division last year,' said Pratihari with a sense of pride.[16]

'The decision to set up a school was taken when Didi and I sat together to weigh and judge if we could bring an institution to life and continue it for all times to come,' he said. 'The logo of the school was designed by Iti (Itishree Murmu). Didi normally visits the school at least four times or more every year,' he explained. Murmu is directly involved in all the decision-making of the institution, which is why, these days, due to her hectic schedule and protocol, Pratihari goes to meet her in New Delhi. 'She is unique and exceptional. In spite of achieving every honour and position in life and braving all challenges, she remains down to earth and humble, and that is an inspiration,' he said.

---

[16] All quotes by Munna Pratihari are from an interview conducted by the author on 11 January 2023.

6
True Stateswoman: Jharkhand Governor

On 18 May 2015, Droupadi Murmu took the oath of office as the governor of Jharkhand and remained in the position till 2021. Besides being the first woman and the first tribal governor of Jharkhand, she was also the first from Odisha to be appointed as the governor of a state. Her term was marked by many important decisions and milestones concerning the passage of bills and assent to amendments.

Her term as governor was also marked by many important and controversial events concerning the marginalized tribals who constitute a majority in Jharkhand. But she remained non-controversial in terms of her understanding of tribal issues and firmness in decision-making. She consistently took up the cudgels for tribal welfare and development but refused to approve certain bills relating to tribals that had already been passed through the Assembly and sought her nod on their amendment. For example, in the case of the amendments to the Chota Nagpur Tenancy (CNT) Act, 1908, and the Santhal Pargana Tenancy (SPT) Act, 1949, Murmu refused to approve the amendments and returned the two Bills to the government with queries. While doing so, she also questioned how they would benefit the tribal masses. She attached the protest petitions, all 192 that the Raj Bhavan had received, to the amendments and returned them.

LAND ISSUES

In 2017, the Raghubar Das-led BJP government in Jharkhand had sought amendments to the CNT Act, 1908, and SPT Act, 1949. These Acts ensured that the use and control of tribal lands remained with the tribals. The amendment to these Acts envisaged giving them the right to use their lands commercially while ensuring that the ownership of land did not change. The government sought these amendments because, according to it, it could not get land for commercial development projects like schools and Anganwadis near the tribal villages. But the National Commission for Scheduled Tribes had discussed the amendments as deviating from the crucial provisions of taking consent of gram sabhas in land transfers, which could not be omitted. It had noted during a meeting in 2016 that if the amendments were put in place, it would violate the PESA Act of 1996 and the Right to Fair Compensation and Transparency in Land Acquisition, Rehabilitation and Resettlement Act, 2013.

Given these larger ramifications, Murmu put the amendment Bills on hold. She convened many meetings and there were proposals from outside the state against them. She later returned the Bills, asking the government to explain the changes the amendments would bring to the larger interest of the tribals. Murmu remained firm in her decision. She stated that land has motherly stature for everyone, particularly the tribals. It cannot be traded off.[1] The RSS is believed to be honest to the tribal cause, which is closely linked to land. Members of the BJP from the tribal-dominated Mayurbhanj district, who have been associated with the cause of the tribals for years, said that when all political parties were distant from the tribal causes, it was the RSS that went into the nooks and crannies to take up the cudgels for the tribals. 'I remember our party members joining them to iron out land-related issues. But this had no local or national media coverage, so there is no documentation of the RSS's work for the tribal communities,' said Nabin Kumar Ram.

People close to Murmu say that her allegiance to the RSS's ideology was strengthened because she could identify with it insofar as her own commitment to fight for the tribal cause was concerned. Born and brought up in challenging situations, she understood the meaning of land for tribals who do not have anything else to sustain them. They believe land is God. During the discussions with various outfits, she made it clear that under no circumstances would the tribals be alienated from their land—their only asset. She was unhappy that the government could not gauge the mood of the tribals in a matter so close to their heart as jal, jungle aur jameen. She consulted legal and tribal affairs experts to study the Bills and understand its nuances as well as ramifications. Only after that did she return the Bills with a suggestion to reconsider.

Ministers during Raghubar Das's Cabinet vouched that Murmu was honest during her administrative term. She kept herself focussed on education in the state during her

---

[1]Datta, Romita, 'Five Unknown Facts about President Droupadi Murmu,' *India Today*, 21 July 2022, https://bit.ly/41PZtok. Accessed on 6 March 2023.

governorship but also put her foot down on matters she thought were not being dealt with fairly by the government.

Then parliamentary affairs minister in Raghubar Das's government, Saryu Roy, worked closely with Murmu and said that she was a governor different from any other that the state had seen. She had strong knowledge of governance but did not interfere in the day-to-day affairs of the government. She was aware and knew where to draw the line but didn't hesitate to take strong action when required, as with returning the Bills. Roy added:

> She was stern in her decisions. Since she was knowledgeable about administration and legislation, she was open to all kinds of exchange of information. She would often keep her doors open for communication with people—official and unofficial. My rapport with her was functional and personal also. Functionally, she has called me many times to her office to discuss matters that she wanted clarity on. She would often call ministers for discussions. She always made sure to learn things that she was not aware of.[2]

She was affectionate and took care of anyone who visited her. Being a soft-spoken person, she never showed anger or critiqued anyone. 'I have seen many governors in my career but she was a cut above the rest. So when the government put an end to her term in Jharkhand, we were all upset. But who knew then that there were larger opportunities for which she would be considered appropriate like presidentship,' Roy narrated.

---

[2] All quotes by Saryu Roy are from an interview conducted by the author on 5 January 2023.

It was on Murmu's insistence that a tribal affairs portfolio was created and a minister given its responsibility during her term. She was never content with only a tribal advisory council, as she thought that the state was populated with tribals and needed a designated person to handle their matters. 'She was aware of the relevant constitutional provisions and, thus, a tribal affairs ministry was constituted and a notification for it issued almost immediately. Gentle to the core, efficient, magnanimous, cordial and strong-minded, there could not have been a better governor in Jharkhand than Madam Murmu,' Roy stated. Roy remained an MLA after his ministerial term but he kept meeting Murmu as and when she desired for consultations or meetings.

In fact, it was Roy who had declared to the press that the amendment Bills to the CNT and SPT Acts passed by the Jharkhand Assembly in November 2016 were returned by the governor on 24 May 2016, citing lack of objectivity. He added that governor wanted both the amendments to be reconsidered. 'The Bills would not be placed for formal cancellation in the Cabinet. It has now been shelved,' he declared.

The Bills were withdrawn in August 2017. But the amendments to the CNT and SPT Acts proved to be the last nail in the coffin of the BJP's electoral prospects. The tribal vote bank shifted away because they thought that the BJP was anti-tribal. In the 2019 elections, the BJP could get only twenty-five out of eighty-one assembly seats while the JMM got thirty. This was in contrast to earlier figures, as the BJP had got thirty-seven seats and the JMM had succeeded in getting only nineteen in 2014.

Newspaper reports were replete with reactions of leaders on the issue. Member of Parliament Sunil Soren hailed Murmu's decision to turn down the Bills, and MP K.V. Singhdeo said that her decision will remain unparalleled.

The political circles were abuzz with rumours that her candidature for the presidential post in 2017 was not taken forward due to her refusal to approve the Bills. But there are others who feel that since Murmu's age was on her side, the NDA wanted to field Ram Nath Kovind first.

The 2017–18 Pathalgadi movement, which was a fallout of the land amendment Acts passed by the government, also proved to be a challenge for Murmu. As the major aim of the movement, the tribals wanted implementation of the PESA Act in totality. They sought Murmu's intervention to stop government interference into the matter using force. The PESA Act, 1996, gives special powers to the gram sabhas in scheduled areas, especially for the management of natural resources. Murmu had convened a meeting with all the traditional tribal chieftains at Birsa Mandap in the Raj Bhavan and listened to their grievances and demands.

The Pathalgadi movement was started by tribals from the Khunti district of Jharkhand to assert their rights, which included their right to a sovereign territory. The word *pathalgadi*, meaning 'carving a stone', was used by the tribals to assert that their wish to restrict the entry of outsiders on the land would be carved in stone.

Soon after, the tribals had strongly objected to the proposed amendment to the tenancy acts, violence erupted. On one occasion, tribals abducted the security personnel of MP Karia Munda, the former deputy speaker of Lok Sabha who belonged to Khunti, as a result of which a police scuffle ensued between the police and tribals. Abram Mundu, a tribal, was killed in the consequent police firing. Criminal cases were filed against more than 200 people, including the tribal rights activist Father Stan Swamy.

Even after Mundu's death in the police firing, CM Das met with resistance in some of the public meeting venues with villagers showing him black flags in Khunti district and hurling shoes at him in Saraikela–Kharsawan district.

Former CM and present Union minister Arjun Munda and MP Kariya Munda, both tribal leaders, were also not in support of the move. Since Das was not a tribal and wanted to amend the land laws pertaining to them, even if he insisted that it would finally benefit them by way of compensation, the step was bound to boomerang.

Given the history of such cases in India, where land belonging to tribals has been proposed to be traded to the investors for infrastructure or mining purposes, it has resulted in tribal uprisings as in the cases of Kalinga Nagar for Tata Steel and Lanjigarh for Vedanta in Odisha. Even Das's domicile policy, announced in 2016, met with resistance.

All the while, Murmu maintained a neutral stance. Her silence was criticized, but she knew where she should intervene and where to draw a line. She followed every action constitutionally and exhorted everyone to have faith in the Constitution. She wanted the tribals to trust the decision. Her clean administration won her the support of her adversaries.

With over one-fourth of the state's population comprising STs, Murmu received immense love from the people during her tenure as the governor. Chief Minister Hemant Soren, being a tribal, was also believed to be close to Murmu.

During her term, Murmu also returned the Private Placement Agency and Domestic Workers Bill, 2017, that sought the revision of penal provisions. She wrote to the government that the penal provision for those found guilty of immoral trafficking in the name of placements must be stringent.

OVERHAULING EDUCATION

As Murmu had promised before taking over as the Jharkhand governor, she laid emphasis on education and approached it first at the level of Lok Adalats, then at the systemic and institutional levels. This two-pronged approach had great results. In a few years, she was instrumental in transforming the education scene in Jharkhand with personal intervention.

As many as 5,000 pending cases of teachers and employees of various educational institutions kept them away from their classes as they had to appear in the courts. These cases were solved through her proactive intervention. She oversaw the creation of the chancellor portal on the website for Jharkhand's universities to address various issues concerning education, higher education institutions and students' matters, including admissions.[3] Moved by the plight of people who had been burdened with litigation for years, she emphasized organizing dozens of Lok Adalats to redress grievances. Particularly for teachers, she advised for the disposal of cases in fast-track courts.

On 10 December 2016, while addressing the third University Lok Adalat, an alternative dispute redressal

---

[3] *Chancellor Portal*, https://bit.ly/3yRqlqS. Accessed on 21 March 2023.

mechanism conducted for teaching and non-teaching staff in Ranchi, Murmu stressed on removing red tapism, which often becomes a hindrance in delivering justice to the people. She stated that Lok Adalats and fast-track courts must be held to ensure faster justice. And taking this forward would be the Jharkhand State Legal Services Authority, she asserted. All land-related issues were prioritized and speedy justice was delivered. Murmu wanted legalities to be done away with on mission mode at primary, middle, high and other department levels.

The then CM Raghubar Das also supported her statement by saying that his government had been taking steps to deliver justice fast to the marginalized and backward people. He had also taken Murmu's wishes forward to ensure that the universities' laws and rules were amended. That year, the Jharkhand government earmarked a budget for computer literacy at the primary level and also started taking steps to focus on higher education. Das assured that education fund allotments were to be increased in the 2017–18 budget, and teachers were to be recruited on fast-track basis.[4]

Hundreds of cases against teachers and educational institutes were disposed of in a day, as Murmu sought help from judges from various courts and brought them together to clear cases quickly. Even Lok Adalats helped a lot.

Addressing a high-level meeting at Raj Bhavan in Ranchi on 24 June 2016, Murmu emphasized that disputes related to promotion, dues and compensation in universities could

---

[4] '3rd University Lok Adalat Held in Ranchi for the Teaching and Non-teaching Staff,' *The Avenue Mail*, https://bit.ly/3Ip7jML. Accessed on 22 February 2023.

be solved easily through Lok Adalats.[5] The Lok Adalat was a better way to provide justice to the people; petitioners did not have to run around courts for long. Hence, the universities could opt for Lok Adalats to solve the matters related to retired teaching and non-teaching staff so that they could get justice early.

Justice D.N. Patel of Jharkhand High Court, who attended the meeting, said that there are provisions for free legal support to citizens in the Constitution of India. He also asserted then that not only the courts, even the vice chancellor had the capacity to dispose of some cases.

Murmu insisted that case-related files must be moved expeditiously and stressed on handling cases of widows, children and physically challenged persons sensitively.

The first University Lok Adalat was organized in the country on 13 May 2012 at Nyaya Sadan, Jharkhand State Legal Services Authority, Ranchi, for the pending as well as pre-litigation matters of the teaching and non-teaching employees of Jharkhand's universities. As many as 149 cases were disposed of and an amount of ₹3.85 crore disbursed.[6] Within ten days, the second University Lok Adalat was organized at the same place where 130 matters were disposed of and ₹2.49 crore disbursed among the beneficiaries.[7]

Murmu was a part of the third exercise that began on 23 June 2016. The adalats turned out to be a pathway of

---

[5]'Use Lok Adalats to Resolve Varsity Issues, Says Guv,' *The Times of India*, 24 June 2016, https://bit.ly/3SOojkA. Accessed on 6 March 2023.
[6]'Lok Adalat Settles 149 University Cases,' *The Times of India*, 14 May 2012, https://bit.ly/3ZHQ0xz. Accessed on 6 March 2023.
[7]'Lok Adalat Leaves 130 Teachers Happy,' *The Telegraph Online*, 23 May 2012, https://bit.ly/3ZrwlCo. Accessed on 6 March 2023.

social engineering by helping people who had long faced legal hassles. 'We are committed to provide them relief,' Justice Dipak Misra stated on 10 December 2016. As many as 5,537 cases were disposed of in one go. An amount of ₹113.58 crore was distributed among 4,910 beneficiaries that day.[8]

It took six months of hard work and a series of high-level meetings to achieve the kind of result that was seen on the day. Appointment letters were handed out to many teachers while those who were deprived of Fifth and Sixth Pay Commission benefits were handed cheques.

Supreme Court judges Dipak Mishra and R. Bhanumati, executive judge P.K. Mohanty, H.C. Mishra, D.N. Patel, Aparesh Kumar Singh, Rajesh Shankar and S.N. Pathak were present on the occasion of the third Lok Adalat.

Being the chancellor of the universities, Murmu went beyond her capacity to change things in various educational institutions and formulating new policies to ensure seamless teaching–learning in them. During her term, the education system saw an overhaul. She personally went to schools and higher education institutions to oversee the academic activities. The problems she had faced in her own experience of education strengthened her resolve to help others get education facilities seamlessly. Education and empowerment of women still stays at that top of her agenda, and she does not mince words while speaking on these issues at various academic institutions or functions as the president of the country.

---

[8]Jha, Sanjeev, 'SC Judge Wants Boost to Culture of Settlement', *The Pioneer*, 11 December 2016, https://bit.ly/3L4y8sV. Accessed on 6 March 2023.

Since education is a sure-shot tool to curb poverty, she ensured that every educational institution had basic infrastructure, their governance was held accountable and a sufficient number of teachers were recruited so that the students did not suffer.

According to the then state education minister and BJP legislator from Kodarma, Neera Yadav, during Murmu's term, the Lok Adalats proved to be a boon. She mentioned:

> Jharkhand saw tremendous improvement, in the education sector particularly, and since I was the education minister, I constantly saw the revolutionary steps she took to bring change in the life of students and institutions. She was the chancellor for universities but I think Murmu is the only exception as a governor who took it upon herself to revolutionize primary, secondary and higher secondary educational institutions during her six years.[9]

A survey conducted in Jharkhand showed that eleven districts were backward as far as girls' education was concerned.[10] These districts did not have any institution to impart education at the higher secondary level; as a result, those wishing to pursue higher education needed to go out of the state to study. As the governor, Murmu made sure that all these districts have degree colleges so that girls

---

[9]All quotes by Neera Yadav are from an interview conducted by the author on 12 January 2023.
[10]Singh, Ayushi, 'The Status of Girls' Education in Jharkhand,' *SSRN*, 3 August 2020, https://bit.ly/3JfYXbY. Accessed on 6 March 2023; 'An Exclusive Interview with India's First Tribal President, Draupadi Murmu by Dr. Itirani Samanta,' YouTube, http://bit.ly/420iZ1w. Accessed on 10 March 2023.

get the chance to study till at least the bachelor's level. In twelve other districts, model co-educational colleges were opened so that girls and boys could study together in their own districts without having to go out. Besides, she was instrumental in opening Kasturba Gandhi Balika Vidyalayas (KGBVs) for the below-poverty-line and downtrodden students who did not have the means to study. A few of these KGBVs admitted students up to Class 8, but she asked the department to immediately upgrade all the schools to have Class 10, and later, Class 12. She wanted to include not only arts but also science and commerce streams in the curriculum so that students could have the freedom to study what they wished to, explained Yadav, who worked closely with Murmu.

In Jharkhand, due to teacher absenteeism and lack of streamlining of processes in day-to-day academic work, a three-year undergraduate course was being completed in five to six years. To address this issue, Murmu exhorted all stakeholders to mend their ways.[11] As the chancellor of the universities, Murmu entirely revamped the systems for admissions, examinations, classes and declaration of results. She called a meeting of everyone concerned to discuss how to set the system straight for the benefit of students.

In just three years, changes started showing. The curriculum got updated and procedural delays stopped. The details of all higher secondary and above institutions were uploaded and updated from time to time on the chancellor's portal. From admissions to results, student strength to faculty ratio and important dates were all

---

[11] 'An Exclusive Interview with India's First Tribal President, Draupadi Murmu by Dr Itirani Samanta,' YouTube, http://bit.ly/420iZ1w. Accessed on 10 March 2023.

available online. More and more colleges were established in various parts of the state.

'We introduced job-oriented vocational training subjects in the school and college curriculum. Since students were good at song and dance, there were courses of fine arts and culture introduced in the universities. There were many who were good at sports and they were channelized accordingly. Today, these sportspersons are making a name [for themselves] nationally and internationally,' said Murmu during one of her interviews.[12]

In twenty-four districts of the state, a total of 302 KGBVs were revived. Murmu intervened in the functioning of residential schools, where there was neither any security nor doctors, and made sure all these facilities were immediately provided. Her timely intervention gave every KGBV a facelift.

On 21 January 2017, addressing more than 1,000 students of Kasturba Gandhi Awasiya Balika Vidyalaya and teachers in Govindpur, around 12 km from Dhanbad, Murmu expressed her desire to see all girls educated. She emphasized in her speech that the progress of a nation depends on how advanced and educated its girls and women are.[13]

Even though Jharkhand was one of the richest states in the country in terms of minerals, forest, water and human resources, the overall development of the state and its people lagged behind many others. Among the development parameters for the state, education, particularly for girls, was not encouraging, and Murmu wanted to change this. She would cite the Kerala model of

---

[12]Ibid.
[13]'Governor Bats for Girl Literacy', *The Telegraph Online*, 22 January 2017, http://bit.ly/407x9Ne. Accessed on 23 March 2023.

education as an example, where the literacy rate was 99 per cent, and stressed on its emulation.

Addressing the girls at KGBV, she said that women have a lot of potential but that needs to be tapped into and urged them to utilize their skills. Maino Majhi, a teacher at one of the KGBVs, said that every word Murmu spoke had an impact on students and staff. 'We used to wait for the day when Madam Governor would visit our school, and the day she came, we were all so inspired by the way she conducted herself,' she said.[14]

When smart classes were started in KGBVs in the Garhwa district, Murmu was the first one to inspect them on 4 October 2016. She also went around the school premises, including classes, labs and hostels. 'She asked teachers to motivate students so that they lead fruitful lives. She made us think of novel ways to teach the children so that their moral fabric is also enhanced and they grow up to be individuals with high morals and character,' remembered Majhi.

Besides, Murmu was insistent on all institutions having proper infrastructure and gym facility, as she felt youngsters need to take care of their fitness.

'I was so enamoured with her personality and the way she worked that I made diaries and cards with her photograph in it to distribute among my associates and followers. And this was much before her becoming the president,' Yadav said.

Another important contribution Yadav remembered Murmu having initiated was the opening of Jharkhand

---

[14] All quotes by Maino Majhi are from an interview conducted by the author on 20 December 2022.

Raksha Shakti University in the state. Yadav said, 'The VCs of the institution are generally retired defence personnel, and students here are trained in many facets, both technical and non-technical, to get into the armed forces. Besides that, the students are also trained in tracking cybercrimes.'

She added, 'The university was established by the Government of Jharkhand on 3 October 2016, and is recognized by the UGC, New Delhi. The first of its kind in Jharkhand and third in the country, the institution offers certificate, diploma and degree courses in the field of police science and internal security.'

Until the new university building becomes operational, the activities of the university are being conducted from the Old Judicial Academy building (the campus of Shri Krishna Institute of Public Administration) situated on Meur's Road, Ranchi. Its permanent campus is being established over a wide area of 75 acres near Khunti, which is around 30 km away from Ranchi city.

When Murmu went to Jharkhand ahead of the presidential elections to seek support, Yadav fondly recollected how they hugged each other. She also recollects one of her friends visiting Murmu at Rashtrapati Bhavan, where the president expressed how protocols of speaking, wearing and conducting herself in particular ways irk her. She wants to remain carefree as a president and meet people as a common person. 'I look forward to her term as president as it would be special. I also want to meet her at Rashtrapati Bhavan soon,' concluded Yadav.

Once, when Murmu visited two girls' schools in Hazaribagh—a centre for the hearing impaired and another school for the mentally challenged—on 8 August 2017, she surprise checked the hostel and kitchen at the

Prathamik Balika Awasiya Vidyalaya at Dipugarha. She was deeply shocked when the students she interacted with failed to name the PM of the country. She asked the teachers to make a list of names of all important personalities of the country and put it up in every classroom.

She also assured the students that she would request the CM to improve the infrastructure in schools. It also became quite usual for the unassuming Murmu to stop at some schools every day to see if all was well.

A BOOST FOR TRIBAL LIVES

Apart from education, health indicators of tribals were also a priority for Murmu. She insisted on the state and central governments working in tandem to give the marginalized their due at least through health welfare schemes. Education is important, and once a tribal person gets educated, he or she will take care of their health concerns as well.

She has been vocal about many other issues concerning the tribal people. She wanted them to be allowed to collect minor forest produce and store it, as against the current limit of storing only 5 kg mahua. She was also openly against outsiders interfering in purchasing minor forest produce from the tribals. According to her, other than the government, no one should interfere in this, as it is the only source of income for tribal people. She expressed concern about the changing governments in the state that had affected its development. There have been as many as ten governments in two decades of Jharkhand's existence.

But she was always positive about changing the lives of the tribals. In Jharkhand, her doors were always open to people. She would hear as many of them as possible and then take up their issues with the government.

The Charan Paduka Yojana introduced in Jharkhand got Murmu's support as well. Footwear was provided to members of the poorest and most marginalized tribal groups in the state for free as part of the scheme. About 100,000 tribals benefitted under the scheme, launched by CM Raghubar Das, in its first phase.

Once, while speaking at Sekkor Premium League organized by Tata Steel's ore, mines and quarries division at Noamundi Sports Stadium in West Singhbhum district in Jharkhand, Murmu emphasized how everyone, including the mining sector, needs to work towards educating tribals.[15] She expressed her concern that they were often taken for granted and cheated in the process because they were uneducated and gullible. Not all of them would get a government job, but education could at least open their eyes to what was good and bad. So, everyone must take steps for their empowerment. She appreciated Tata Steel for their tribal-friendly programmes in terms of providing livelihood, education and awareness about saving the girl child and simultaneously promoting tribal culture through their corporate social responsibility activities. Murmu expressed her happiness at tribal sports being preserved and not becoming extinct. 'Traditional tribal sports like Kati, Sekkor, Chhur, Bahu Chor and Ramdel played by the Santal and Ho communities of Jharkhand are on the path of revival and that is so heartening,' she said at the event.

Her Jharkhand term, however, never overshadowed

---

[15]'Education Gives Right Direction in Life: Jharkhand Guv,' *Business Standard*, 13 June 2017, https://bit.ly/3L1Vdwk. Accessed on 6 March 2023.

her concerns for her native place and constituency. Amid her responsibilities at Ranchi, she kept track of the well-being of the people back home with equal zeal and wanted to ensure the development of the villages in her home district.

Ishwar Chandra Mishra and Shyam Charan were colleagues at the Bank of India but posted in different branches. Mishra, as a bank officer, was reformative by principle, which earned him a lot of goodwill among people. Murmu, too, was impressed by him and wanted him to grant loans to villagers and launch digital banking schemes in remote villages. He obliged. 'Our purpose was that banking facilities should be available to all. So I was not doing anything great, I was just ensuring that villages like Uparbeda, which were untouched by banking facilities, get all banking help as early as possible. And Madam Governor's instructions were good enough to be carried forward,' Mishra remembered.

In 2017, after Mishra was transferred to Keonjhar zone, which had thirteen Odisha districts under its fold, Murmu called him and expressed her concern about uplifting Uparbeda and other smaller villages nearby. She wanted the people there to lead a hassle-free life where they could get money to start a business or invest in vocational training or agriculture at lower rates of interest so that they can pay back the principal amount. 'Please help them with banking facilities and provide loans to the needy so that they can do something better to earn a livelihood,' she asked Mishra. As Mayurbhanj was under the Keonjhar banking jurisdiction, Mishra quickly agreed to do whatever was required. This was around the time when Bank of India was getting into the digitization of villages in a big way. Mishra stated:

> I immediately instructed my team to start work in Uparbeda village. We did extensive data collection and, to the entire literate population, we provided provisions of opening bank accounts, getting debit cards and sanctioning loans to those who wished to invest in any livelihood option. We also set up training camps for women to learn stitching and granted them loans to buy a sewing machine that could help them earn.

Mishra added that the loan facilitation was done on a differential rate of interest of 4 per cent only. 'Loans were provided to even those who wished to take up mushroom cultivation,' Mishra says.

As it is, Mishra was known as an efficient bank officer by colleagues and senior officials, and as a human being, he has always been appreciated by Murmu for his prompt response to all her concerns. She also asked Mishra to ensure that villagers who had benefitted under the Pradhan Mantri Ujjwala Yojana were lent help in getting gas cylinders or stoves because most did not have them. He arranged a grant of loans for such people in the village. Additionally, he went from Bhubaneswar to Rairangpur in 2022 and personally oversaw the puja and food distribution at the SLS School, Pahadpur, so that everything was celebrated in a proper way. 'Since I am like family, Madam had called me to say that I must be there to ensure the event was organized in the usual way as she was unable to come due to her hectic schedule,' Mishra stated.

He met Murmu on 19 June 2022 at Rairangpur, two days ahead of her nomination for the presidential election, to invite her for his son's wedding in July. Mishra asked her about the news doing rounds that she was being considered for the top position of the country and whether there was any veracity to the rumours. 'She said that she did not know if there was any such plan and that she had never aspired for anything but was ready to take up any responsibility given to her by the party. She asked God to give her the strength to serve her country,' Mishra recollected.

She immediately agreed to the wedding invitation, but soon after her nomination and election, she called up Mishra, expressing her inability to attend the function. 'She called me up to say that she could not make it with so much protocol around her. However, she met my son and daughter-in-law when she came to Bhubaneswar on her first visit to Odisha after becoming the president. She blessed them and gave them gifts,' Mishra further said.

Murmu expressed her gratitude to her party's leadership for being given the governor's position to do something good for the state. Before returning to Odisha, she said:

> PM Modi has always stressed on sabka saath, sabka vikas, and he has lived every word of it. He has always cared for the sentiments of all people and wanted to give people from the underprivileged sections a chance to be in the mainstream and work towards progress and development. I am fortunate to have worked as the governor of a state that not only shares a common border with my native place but also has similar culture and lifestyle.[16]

---

[16] 'An Exclusive Interview with India's First Tribal President, Draupadi Murmu by Dr. Itirani Samanta,' YouTube, http://bit.ly/420iZ1w. Accessed

A GRACIOUS HOST

Madam President's friends remember that when they got together to organize an alumni meet in Bhubaneswar, they did not have the courage to invite her, as she was the governor then. 'We did not have the budget and possibly could not have organized it in a hotel where the governor of a state could visit,' recollected her friend Dangi. Since the budget was shoestring, they pooled in money to just barely manage the event. 'But we decided to invite her. When she agreed, our dilemma doubled because we had to choose a good venue. Then we started scouting for a good place where the governor could sit with us, speak and eat. All preparations were done but, unfortunately, her plan with us got cancelled due to some official work,' said friend Chinmayee.

In a few months, however, some six to seven friends of Murmu were invited by her to the Ranchi Raj Bhavan. Chinmayee fondly recollected:

> We were upbeat and agreed immediately. Though my son is in the armed forces and posted in Ranchi, I decided to stay with Murmu at the sprawling house of the governor. The grand reception and hospitality were simply unforgettable. She ensured that we all had a good trip, visited all tourist places and enjoyed good food during our stay. One day, she accompanied us to move around in the lawns of the Raj Bhavan to enjoy the beauty of the blooms and well-chiselled lawns.

The friends were in awe of the grandeur of the governor's house—from the palatial rooms to décor to food.

---

on 10 March 2023.

Chinmayee recollected that everything was impressive.

On the day of their departure from Ranchi, Murmu gave them saris and other gifts besides *arisapitha* (an Odia fried pancake) that she had specifically asked her sister-in-law Sakramani, who used to stay with her in the governor's house, to prepare. Chinmayee said:

> We were surprised to see a wide variety of food on the dining table, though it was all made without onion and garlic. Her sister-in-law also ensured that we eat 'mathasaag', specific to Rairangpur that she had fetched just before we went to visit Murmu. We were later told that Droupadi enjoys her home food so much, and particularly saag, that the leafy sprigs are specifically picked up by her sister-in-law whenever she visits home.

Dangi, who was also a part of the group, said she ate the saag from her village after twenty-six years.

'Sakramani was at her native place when Murmu specifically requested her to return to the Raj Bhavan ahead of her group of friends,' Chinmayee remembered. With almost royal hospitality and visits to places around the state, the seven friends were treated to the best vacation of their life.

Sakramani Tudu mostly stays with Murmu and takes care of her personal guests and friends wherever she is posted. Even now, she is with Madam President at the Rashtrapati Bhavan.

Delha Soren also visited Murmu at the governor's house in Jharkhand on special invitation. Accorded special treatment at Raj Bhavan, Soren remembered having been escorted to many places in the state for sight-seeing and also being taken care of with all comforts, like a state guest. 'She gifted me a flower-bearing plant called Ashoka. I have it at my house in Adarsha Vihar in Bhubaneswar now, and it's in full bloom. I wish she would come to my house someday to see what a splendid bloom the tree bears,' said Soren.

'Like Didi, I never liked protocol. So, whenever she invited me to the Raj Bhavan, I preferred staying somewhere else because I could not stick to so much protocol,' reminisced Ranjan Patel. He has also been a pillar of strength for Murmu in her good and bad times. 'There are instances when I have needed Didi's help and she has made sure my work was done. I was filled with pride while escorting her to the Raj Bhavan from Rairangpur to Ranchi. I was then the party in-charge for the state of Jharkhand and was equally known to Raghubar Das too,' revealed Patel.

Raj Bhavan staffers in Ranchi said that Murmu would unfailingly get up before dawn to perform her daily spiritual rituals, including an offering of water to the peepul tree in the complex. As most of the food in the Raj Bhavan was cooked in a sattwik manner, the guests too were served the same food. There was a strict restriction on non-vegetarian food on the premises. Murmu, too, used to go to the kitchen at times to make something special during festivals. She used to guide the cooking staff on how to make some dishes tastier.

Mishra reminisced, 'Since I loved non-vegetarian food, she would request some of her staff staying outside the Raj Bhavan to prepare good mutton and feed me.' She was irritated at always being in the midst of a security cover. She did not like binding protocol. While she used to walk in the lawns of the Raj Bhavan, the security personnel would follow her closely. 'If she wished to speak to someone while walking, she would ask her security staff to stay a little further away so that she could speak openly. And as far as her courtesy is concerned, it is unparalleled,' Mishra averred.

As per the Santal tradition, Tudus professionally are singers and dancers. Many videos of Her Excellency shaking a leg in sync with the other women, hand-in-hand, waving a fan in the other hand and maintaining a rhythm are popular on YouTube.[17] During one programme while she was the governor, she did not hesitate to perform with a group of dancers, which was widely appreciated. The song she danced on underwent many versions due to its popularity and became a rage on YouTube soon after.

During her entire term as governor, her daughter and grandchildren stayed with her. Even though Itishree was a bank employee, she could manage to get a transfer to be with her mother.

PEOPLE'S OWN

One of the trademarks of Murmu's personality is the impression she leaves on the people she meets. The many people she interacted with during her tenure as the governor have a lot to say about her.

Yadav remembered the days she worked with Murmu as 'golden'. She felt she was working with her elder sister as she got Murmu's love and affection as younger sibling. She said:

---

[17] 'When Governor Droupadi Murmu Danced with Villagers in 2018,' YouTube, https://bit.ly/3FEfTXr. Accessed on 21 March 2023.

I have never seen such a personality in my life, who, after occupying such important positions in the country, has no sense of pride or haughtiness. She has always been a grassroots worker and grounded. I was a first-time minister during her term and I got so much guidance from her in all the work I did then. I have approached her many times for help and she has immediately stood by me. *Woh aisi mahila hai jo atmiya dhang se har kaam karti hai* [she is the kind of woman who puts her heart into all she does]. 'Simple, sober and efficient' best describe Madam Murmu.

Murmu had an amicable relationship with CM Hemant Soren who met her at regular intervals, even during the peak of Covid. Chief Minister Soren stated that he visited her on 26 June 2020 to keep her informed about the status of Covid in the state. He last informed her of the same when Jharkhand had 626 active cases and the government was about to lift some of the restrictions.[18]

As per a statement released by the Raj Bhavan, Soren also spoke to Murmu about the government's commitment to ensuring no one remains hungry in the state. 'The government is making efforts to bring back *pravasis* [migrant workers] as per their desire. Awareness is being created regarding the lockdown guidelines to contain the spread of the coronavirus, Soren told the governor,' the release stated.[19]

---

[18] 'COVID-19: CM Soren Meets Governor Draupadi Murmu in Ranchi,' YouTube, https://bit.ly/3TyECm1. Accessed on 23 March 2023.
[19] 'Soren Meets Murmu, Apprises Her of Govt's Efforts in Fighting COVID-19,' *Business Standard*, 14 May 2020, http://bit.ly/3JAyoxj. Accessed on 23 March 2023.

Praising the Soren government's proactive role during Covid, Murmu, during the Budget Session of the fifth Jharkhand Assembly, which started on 27 February 2021, highlighted the achievements of the government in her forty-four-minute address.[20]

Soren has openly acknowledged her contribution to the state during her gubernatorial stint. He termed her as one of the most efficient and active governors in the country. She personally looked into many aspects for the growth and development of the state, particularly in the field of education.

Ex-CM Raghubar Das nurses no ill feelings for Murmu despite the fact that she returned the amendment Bills, putting his leadership at stake halfway through his term. Rather, he feels happy to have worked with her and learnt many things. 'She was gentle, simple and a hard worker. A symbol of *antyodaya*—the welfare of the people at the bottom of the pyramid—Murmu led a life of common people even as the governor. She has all the qualities to inspire girls to fight for their rights,' said Das.

She often laid emphasis on education and, because of her, the Faculty of Tribal and Regional Languages at Ranchi University was established.

On the day Das resigned in 2019, Murmu asked him to be the caretaker CM till the new government was formed. By then, though, Das had not known the results of the elections. He was, however, aware of the defeat staring at him in Jamshedpur (East) seat as a fallout of the tribals' dissatisfaction. But he agreed to be in charge as long as the government was formed.

---

[20] 'Guv Praises Govt's Covid Fight, Welfare Schemes,' *The Pioneer*, 27 February 2021, http://bit.ly/3LF2B0R. Accessed on 23 March 2023.

Despite differences of opinion on various acts, Murmu and Das shared a good rapport and had many things in common. While both were workaholics, the two also had sattwik food at their residences. Unofficially, too, both leaders met many times at the Raj Bhavan over dinner or lunch. The staff at the CM's office and residence as well as at the Raj Bhavan had a tough time dishing out delicacies that would be prepared without use of onion and garlic, let alone non-vegetarian items. Senior BJP leader Ranjan Patel mentions the working styles of both the leaders. 'As the CM, Das would ensure all the files on his table were handled on the same day. He would spend most of his time in office and was not one to carry any work home. Similarly, Didi, too, was never one to procrastinate any work pending with her,' he said.

'She is exceptional,' Das said. 'Once I promised at a public meeting that I would learn Santali and speak it. I forgot about it, but she remembered and reminded me every time I met her. She is very committed to the tribal cause and preserving its culture,' he added.

Former JMM MLA Prahlad Purty spoke greatly about her tenure during her governorship. She was approachable to even her political opponents during her terms as minister or governor.

When Murmu was a minister, Purty won the Bahalda seat during the 2004–09 term as an MLA. 'Didi had such a relationship with me that she did not contest the 2009 elections from Rairangpur, leaving the seat for me. She considered me as her younger brother. But, unfortunately, the JMM did not let me contest from the seat,' recalled Purty.

During her term, Murmu did a lot for her constituency—from roads to buildings to bridges. Purty stated:

> She is highly respected for her contribution in making Santali script a part of the Eighth Schedule of the Constitution. I am an Adivasi too, but my surname is a little different, so most people mistake me as a non-Adivasi. We have fought for the cause of Adivasis in general. Her term as the governor of Jharkhand was highly appreciated even by the JMM as she did a lot of reformative works there.

He said that to support Murmu and assist her in campaigning, he left the JMM for a while. 'I wanted to be with Didi when she contested MP elections to support her in campaigning,' he added.

MOVING ON

Murmu's term as governor was to end on 18 May 2020, but was extended by a year in the wake of the pandemic until Ramesh Bais took over on 16 July 2021. On the day of her farewell, CM Soren, with his wife Kalpana Murmu Soren, saw her off at the Ranchi airport. The Soren couple also used to courtesy visit her at the Rashtrapati Bhavan. As per sources close to her family, Mrs Soren is a distant relative of Murmu.

When Murmu's chartered plane landed on her home turf, she received a rousing reception at Rairangpur. But soon, she stepped into her work as usual.

She rejoined the BJP once again, as she had had to forego her affiliation to the party after assuming the post of the governor. To serve people in a proactive way, she also wanted to get into politics once again, even though her decision was criticized by many. She felt that there was no rule or law to prevent one from joining a party or contesting an election after having served in a constitutional position. There have been many instances in the past where leaders have come back to their parties to work for the people after their term in constitutional positions. The decision, she felt, should be based on the individual's ideology.

'A statesman extraordinaire is how I would describe her personality in two words,' senior BJP leader Surama Padhy said about Murmu. Stating that there could not have been anyone more appropriate than Murmu to take the position of the president, she described her personality as a combination of polite, patient and perfect. 'Her rise has been slow and gradual and completely in sync with the democratic process. She has been a normal person like any of us, she never had a roadmap charted nor decided anything in advance. It is sheer hard work and dedication that took her to the position. For me, she was and will always remain an icon,' Padhy said.

Murmu has been working for the people when she was active in politics and otherwise as well. 'I believe that unless one gets into active politics, solving people's problems isn't as easy,' she had once said on being questioned about why she wanted to join politics again.[21] The people always saw her as their leader, one who would stand by them, come

---

[21] 'Kholakotha | Earlier Discussion with Former Jharkhand Governor Draupadi Murmu,' YouTube, https://bit.ly/3JVr0hi. Accessed on 21 March 2023; 'Exclusive Interview with Former Governor of Jharkhand, Draupadi Murmu,' YouTube, https://bit.ly/402BRvB. Accessed on 21 March 2023.

what may. This trust of the people in her remained intact even when she was away as the governor of Jharkhand. Addressing their problems was paramount, and Murmu felt that she needed to step into active politics again to do whatever work the party gave her. Indebted to her sangathan for giving her so much in life, she wanted to give back to it by way of service to the people. While not keen on contesting elections for the Assembly, Murmu was certainly open to getting into the MP elections or nominations to the Upper House of Parliament. She did not realize then that there were many important roles cut out for her in a year's time.

7

Fifteenth President, Her Excellency

'Johar! Namaste! I humbly greet all the countrymen from this holy Parliament, a symbol of the hopes and aspirations and rights of all the citizens of India. Your affinity, your trust and your support will be my greatest strength in fulfilling this new responsibility.'[1]

These were the words of the country's fifteenth president, Droupadi Murmu, immediately after she was administered the oath of office on 21 July 2022.

Her first address to the nation began with 'Johar', a tribal salutation signifying victory for all living and non-living beings, and she expressed gratitude to all who chose to make her the president. Speaking about the coincidences that initiated her tenure as the president, she said that her political career began when India was celebrating fifty years of Independence. It is a coincidence that she is beginning her role as the president when India is celebrating seventy-five years of Independence—Azadi Ka Amrit Mahotsav.

'Since I have been given this important position, I

---

[1] '"First President to Be Born in Independent India": Here Is What Draupadi Murmu Said in Her First Address to the Nation after Swearing-In', *OpIndia*, 25 July 2022, https://bit.ly/3IndmS5. Accessed on 23 February 2023.

will strive to serve the nation to the best of my capability, dedication and devotion,' Murmu stated in the first tweet from the President of India handle after assuming charge.[2]

Prime Minister Narendra Modi and top leaders from various parties including many CMs attended the swearing-in ceremony. Among the political luminaries, PM Modi was the first one to reflect on the journey of Madam President as an able administrator. 'Smt. Droupadi Murmu Ji has devoted her life to serving society and empowering the poor, downtrodden as well as the marginalised. She has rich administrative experience and had an outstanding gubernatorial tenure. I am confident she will be a great President of our nation,' the PM tweeted.[3] 'Millions of people, especially those who have experienced poverty and faced hardships, derive great strength from the life of Smt. Droupadi Murmu Ji. Her understanding of policy matters and compassionate nature will greatly benefit our country,' he wrote in another tweet.[4]

Eleven years after Indian Independence, when President Murmu aka Putti was born, the impact of Independence had not been felt in the hinterlands. She was born in a free India but it was not free from the shackles of poverty. Development was a far cry. Not every village had a school and not every girl the opportunity to study. In spite of adverse situations and challenges, she was firm in her resolve to make a difference. She had the support of her

---

[2]@rashtrapatibhvn, *Twitter*, 25 July 2022, 10.34 a.m., https://bit.ly/40kU1Zc. Accessed on 21 March 2023; author's translation.
[3]@narendramodi, *Twitter*, 21 June 2022, 9.52 a.m., https://bit.ly/40I rNDd. Accessed on 21 March 2023.
[4]@narendramodi, *Twitter*, 21 June 2022, 9.55 a.m., https://bit.ly/3JWc4zF. Accessed on 21 March 2023.

father, who wanted her to break free and write her own future.

Murmu did. She scripted her story with conviction, without foreseeing that she would finally be installed in the topmost position of the country and become an inspiration to millions of others. Marked by successes and losses, both personal and professional, Murmu, as the first Adivasi woman to adorn the seat, will remind every Indian of the steely resolve she has and that in a true democracy, people, irrespective of their social standing, can carve their way to the top.

Odisha CM Naveen Patnaik said it was the 'biggest moment for every Odia' and that he was fortunate to have been part of that 'golden moment in history'.[5]

Murmu's elevation to the topmost position of the country has not only signified women's emancipation in the absolute sense, it has also started making an impact among all sections of the society. 'The status of the country's indigenous, marginalised tribal community, undoubtedly, stands elevated through Murmu. The BJP will get an electoral benefit. It may not be a substantial one, but will be noticeable in electoral politics,' R.K. Verma, senior political researcher and member of Indian Institute of Public Administration, said to *The New Indian Express*.[6]

---

[5]Mohanty, Debabrata, 'Murmu's Swearing-In Was Biggest Moment for Every Odia: Patnaik,' *The Hindustan Times*, 29 July 2022, https://bit.ly/3xNpM0U. Accessed on 23 February 2023.

[6]Thakur, Rajesh Kumar, 'Tribal Woman Murmu as Prez Pick to Yield Poll Dividends,' *The New Indian Express*, 23 June 2022, https://bit.ly/3EUPqET. Accessed on 6 June 2023.

POLITICAL RELEVANCE: A FACE FOR THE TRIBALS

The BJP had lacked a tribal face to be projected in states that have a good representation of tribal population and the party took a well-thought decision to take its sabka saath, sabka vikas agenda a notch forward. In Jharkhand, West Bengal, Gujarat and Rajasthan, where votes sway as per tribal sentiments, the party has been able to favourably sway them with Murmu, who will play a big role in winning their trust.

Reacting to remarks on President Murmu's elevation as only a tactic of the BJP, party spokesperson Shehzaad Poonawala said that such comments are extremely unfortunate and cynical. He stated:

> Even in the 2019 election, the BJP did well in the tribal communities or ST seats. It is an idea of empowerment of the tribal community. It had started under the NDA-I government under Vajpayee ji when a tribal affairs ministry started in 1999. Then a National Commission for Scheduled Tribes was created in 2003. Allocation of projects linked to tribal communities increased from ₹21,000 crore to ₹86,000 crore in the last few years. In all the schemes introduced by PM Modi like Pradhan Mantri Aawas Yojana, Ayushman Bharat Yojana or Pradhan Mantri MUDRA Yojana, the maximum beneficiaries are people in the ST communities. The allocation of budget for the Eklavya Model Schools has increased, and so have scholarships.[7]

Poonawala referred to the District Mineral Fund started by the Modi government to give a boost to tribal development

---

[7] All quotes by Shehzaad Poonawala are from an interview conducted by the author on 29 January 2023.

activities. Around 30 per cent of the fund is used for the development of tribal areas. Around ₹1,000 crore were allocated to celebrate the tribal culture during Azadi Ka Amrit Mahotsav so that our tribals can be empowered, he stated. 'A lot of tribal leaders' contribution is being recognized. Notably, tribal icon Birsa Munda's birthday on 15 November was celebrated as Janjatiya Gourav Diwas and it is a reflection of the narrative of social empowerment that is being taken forward by the PM Modi-led government,' Poonawala asserted.

The government's aim in the last eight-and-a-half years has been to deliver genuine justice and social welfare to all those who deserve it. A new class of people, *labharthi*s [beneficiaries], has been created, and there is an effort to give some kind of relief to some sections of people based on political calculations, while genuine justice and social welfare for all those who deserve them on the parameter of backwardness have begun. Whether it is the 12 crore toilets built, 9.5 crore cylinders given under the Ujjwala Scheme, 3.5 crore houses built under the Awas Yojana, 6.5 crore Nal Se Jal Yojana tap water connections provided, ₹50 crore disbursed under Ayushman Bharat cover, free healthcare up to ₹5 lakh provided for treatment, ₹2.51 lakh crore disbursed as small business loans under the MUDRA Yojana or about ₹4,606 crore supplied as loans to over 45 lakh beneficiaries under SVANidhi, 45 crore bank accounts have been created—these are for labharthis who are people on the fringes or marginalized. They are reaping the benefits of social justice and welfare. In the whole narrative of social welfare, one of the more important steps is the representation that is being given to the SC/

ST communities. In Uttar Pradesh, if you see, many ST candidates have won on BJP tickets, be it in 2019 General Elections or Gujarat elections.[8] Poonawala explained:

> The important aspect of the election of Murmu ji is that she is somebody who comes from a humble background and challenging socio-economic circumstances, but rises to become an MLA, minister, governor and performs well, and is chosen on the basis of merit. Therefore, her receiving the opportunity to lead as the president of India is just a reflection of choosing a people's president.

In Murmu's stint as the first tribal governor in a politically volatile Jharkhand (which saw ten governments in twenty years), achievements like completing a full term and a year more and spearheading reforms in the state speak of her dedication, administrative prowess and ability to stand firm even in the face of adversities. As a tribal and a woman, Murmu represents two of the most neglected sections of Indian society. Besides being a symbol of empowerment, Murmu's election as the president is an apt tribute to the sacrifice of tribal freedom fighters like Birsa Munda, Tantya Bhil, Umaji Naik, Tirot Singh, Gunda Dhur and Tilka Manjhi. With gender equality being paramount for achieving the 2030 Sustainable Development Goals (SDGs) and the fight of tribals for their rights over jal, jungle aur jameen continuing since ages, there could not have been a better way to address both the issues in one strike for the BJP-led government.

---

[8]'Election Results: How BJP Is Performing in SC/ST Seats,' *The Times of India*, 23 May 2019, http://bit.ly/3Zb04i6. Accessed on 23 March 2023.

The BJP national vice president Baijayant 'Jay' Panda said that President Murmu's term has already begun sending a strong message, not only across the length and breadth of India but globally as well. 'Tribals and women are especially jubilant, but the hopes and dreams that she has inspired cuts across all sections of society, such as [the] youth, who see in her a living embodiment of a New India where anyone can achieve success,' he said. Attributing her elevation to the top position as an emblem of the BJP's slogan 'Sabka saath, sabka vikas, sabka vishwas, sabka prayas', Panda said that she demolishes several orchestrated campaigns against the government today. 'Most importantly, her mature, wise, firm, yet soft spoken, demeanour is winning hearts and inspiring confidence,' he stressed.[9]

If the 2022 Gujarat poll results are anything to go by, after Murmu's election, the BJP set a record by clinching 156 out of 182 seats (while the Congress won seventeen), a record seventh time in a row. 'The results were undeniably astounding. It is not only me, but the entire politically aware mass would vouch for the impact her election had on the tribal voters,' said Nabin Kumar Ram.

Knowing well that tribals would play a prominent role in these elections, Arvind Kejriwal's Aam Aadmi Party (AAP) made concerted efforts to win the community that nearly constitutes 15 per cent of Gujarat's population. He tied up with the Bhartiya Tribal Party of the state's prominent tribal leader, Chhotubhai Vasava, but could not make a dent in the BJP's share.

The effects of nominating Murmu are still unfolding, albeit gradually. The elevation of Murmu from the

---

[9] All quotes by Jay Panda are from an interview conducted by the author on 6 March 2023.

grassroots to the topmost position has certainly sent a positive indication to the tribals across the country. Former member of the Tribal Advisory Council, Ratan Tirkey, who worked with Murmu closely when she was the governor, said that she will be a strong voice to represent tribals.

If the Adivasi National Convention Committee, Jharkhand, expresses hope that their demands for ST status for many unrecognized communities will be granted by Murmu, the Adivasi Sengel Abhiyan Tribal Empowerment Campaign, led by Salkhan Murmu, also feels their *sengel* [empowerment] movement will bear fruit.[10] They are hopeful that their long-standing demands to recognize Sarna as a religion and enumerate it with other religious categories in the next census will be fulfilled. The movement is on in 250 districts of five states. Most tribal bodies are confident that the time for their betterment has come and they will meet the president sometime soon to take their cause forward.

National coordinator of Adivasi Samanwaya Manch Bharat, Father Nicholas Barla, wants to meet the president and urge her to make sure that the provisions mandated in the Constitution are implemented in letter and spirit. 'She shares our concerns as she is an Adivasi and also comes from a background that is common to most tribals. It is a golden time for tribals as the president is one of us and everyone is pinning hope that she will take steps to protect tribal and legislative rights,' he said.[11]

---

[10] 'Tribals Pin Hope on Droupadi Murmu for Empowerment, "Sarna Code",' *The Economic Times*, 25 July 2022, https://bit.ly/3L3v3cm. Accessed on 6 March 2023.
[11] Quote by Father Nicholas Barla from an interview conducted by the author on 21 December 2022

President Murmu will prove to be the voice of the Adivasi community and an ambassador of Jharkhand's Santali culture, said former Jharkhand CM and BJP national vice president Raghubar Das during a celebration for the occasion of Murmu's historic election as the fifteenth President. Das said that he had worked with Murmu when she was the governor of Jharkhand. She had impressed one and all with her simplicity and hard work. 'Droupadi Murmu ji leads a simple life. Girls, particularly Adivasis, would be inspired by her to fight for their rights,' he said.

Ranjan Patel, a senior BJP leader, expressed his wish for many smaller tribal communities to be accorded the status that has eluded them with Didi at the helm. He said:

> Bhuyanra Adivasis of Odisha are landless primitive tribes. They are neither educated nor have any development programmes reaching them. Similarly, many other tribes have also been left out of the ST status. These people must be considered an integral part of the state and the country, and their needs should now be fulfilled on priority. I would wish Didi to address the concerns of these tribes so that they can also participate in nation building.

The academia feels that President Murmu's election assumes significance at this point in time when India is redefining itself to the world. 'Her election asserted the tribal identity like never before,' said Jyotirmayee Tudu, an assistant professor of public administration in Utkal University.

At a time when India is in the 'phase out structure', where the older norms are paving way for new, minority communities like the tribals should be equitably represented. And that is exactly what the NDA government has done. They have reflected the idea that tribal voices must be heard. 'This appointment will go a long way in addressing issues of social justice. It is a symbol of the social justice agenda which assures adequate representation of the marginalized sections,' Tudu explained, adding that those who have heard Madam President speak at some events, particularly on Constitution Day, must be aware she does not mince words. 'She speaks from the heart; she can call a spade a spade. Experience matters, and coming from a backward area, the kind of exposure she has had in all her roles can only bring in her expertise to important issues,' Tudu said.

Tudu belongs to Udala from Mayurbhanj district. Since she had left her hometown for her education, she had been disconnected from her family traditions and rituals, she said. 'But now I feel that I should at least integrate these things into the curriculum and present a case study through academia so that the uniqueness and diversity of the tribes in general and Santals in particular can be preserved,' she stated. Expressing hope that people like Murmu, who have been elevated to such a position, can inspire many others to be proud of their tribal roots, she believes that tribes being given what is rightfully theirs according to the Constitution can lead to cultural preservation. 'Madam President can help propagate our life and culture like none other,' she added.

Most of the tribal-dominated districts with reserved seats are currently being contested by educated people. The parties, too, are looking for people from the community who are educated enough to take the mantle forward. Tudu explained:

Madam Murmu is a bright example. From the time she was educated enough to teach in a school and then went on to become a minister, governor and now president, she set the tone for everyone in the community. Because of a lack of access to education, she moved out of her village. Even I moved to places where education was accessible. Now, many people from the tribes come out of their villages to urban settings. This is more evident in the Northeast.

What does she expect from the president of the country? Tudu responded:

I look with positive hope that Sarna as a religion gets an identity. We do not want to be one of the 'other' in the category of religions. Tribal feelings and cultural practices must be taken into consideration in the urban space. We do not find a Jaher, which is so integral to our culture, anywhere in the urban areas. I am sure Madam Murmu always took up the cause of tribals and she will keep doing it not only for Santals, but for tribes in general.

The president of the Jharkhand-based Kendriya Sarna Samiti, Bablu Munda, who wishes to meet President Murmu at the Rashtrapati Bhavan, felt that she will be instrumental in giving Sarna the status of a religion during her term. Munda added that a year-and-a-half ago, the Jharkhand Assembly passed a resolution asking the central government to recognize Sarna, whose followers worship nature, as a religion and codify it for census enumeration, he added.

A DAUGHTER LOOKS BACK

Itishree, who was posted in the Bhubaneswar branch of the UCO Bank and was on leave during Murmu's nomination, has currently taken a transfer to New Delhi to be by her mother's side. She has two daughters—one is around two years old while the other is seven to eight months old.

On her mother's election, Itishree feels that it should have been a unanimous selection instead of an election. 'My mother is someone who is fair and balanced as a constitutional head and that was proved during her term as the governor. So I wish all parties could have supported her in becoming the fifteenth president of the country,' said Itishree in an interview. She wants more and more people to know of her mother's life, trials and tribulations, her commitment to work and dutifulness that have made her what she is today.[12] She added:

> Given the humble background that my mother comes from, she has dedicated her life to serving the poor and the marginalized. She has never boasted of her achievements or struggles; she prefers a low profile but was always among people. Her party workers and supporters would vouch for how she dedicated herself to serving the poor and being with the people. Her hard work and integrity are the two major factors that catapulted her to the highest position of the country.

---

[12] 'Presidential Poll: Draupadi Murmu to File Nomination Today, Discussion with Her Daughter Itishree,' YouTube, https://bit.ly/3LKeLW9. Accessed on 23 March 2023.

Giving her mother's example of patience and perseverance, Itishree remembered the dark times the family had to face. But she said that she found her mother completely in control of circumstances and never getting upset, annoyed or angry. Itishree believes that with her strong willpower and determination, she has overcome many challenges, both personal and professional.

Her simple way of life has been appreciated by all who have come in touch with her, and her family is no exception. Itishree remembered how Murmu, during her MLA stint, travelled overnight by bus to Rairangpur and returned to Bhubaneswar so that she could be with her constituents and be present at the Assembly as and when required. She was never fussy about food or clothing. 'And she always wanted us to follow in her footsteps to remain grounded and never hanker after high standard of living,' said Itishree. She explained:

> My mother is like an open book. She mingles with one and all. She does not nurse any grudges or ill will towards anyone, even though she knows that some people have tried to harm her. She has been rewarded by the party because she has worked hard. She has been the most polite person, which has won her students' love, parents' respect and the party's trust. It was her popularity as a teacher that made her win elections at a later stage.

For Itishree, there could not be a better inspiration than the president of the country. 'She is an inspiration for many others as well. Her life is a lesson to all who feel that no one can rise in life without amenities. She has become the hope of all deprived people; they, too, can succeed if they try hard. She has done it despite all odds,' she said, with a sense of pride and fulfilment.

During the period when the family lost its members one after another, Itishree was with her mother and found her gathering the pieces of her life with much difficulty. She referred to her mother as powerful from within, with strong conviction and enough willpower to take the world head on. 'We stood with each other and remained strong,' she said.

She narrated how her mother remembers her father and brothers, particularly on special occasions when she wants to share her achievements. 'For someone who entered politics at a time when it was considered a male bastion, particularly since she had no godfather, she could achieve all this because of her diligence and commitment to do good and her relationship with people and my father stood by her,' Itishree stated.

As she was seeing off her mother at the Bhubaneswar airport when she went to file nominations on 22 June 2022, Itishree commented, 'Who knew Rairangpur? People would search the Internet to find where this place on earth existed. Now, even a place as remote as Uparbeda is etched in history due to her. I cannot be thankful enough to the people who have trusted her and God for bestowing her with the power to work for the people.'

Discussing whether this constitutional position will change her own life in any way in the interview, she said, 'Of course, I wanted to shift to New Delhi to be with my mother. She would need me to be with her to give moral support. At least she will be happy that her only child is with her.'

According to Itishree, until Murmu's security was tightened, restrictions were imposed and the protocol was laid, Murmu met each and every one who reached to congratulate her.

Ishwar Mishra describes how she prefers to speak from the heart instead of being bound by the protocol of speaking from a script. 'She is well-read and has gained extensive knowledge on the present-day situation of the country. When she speaks impromptu, it is from the heart and it touches people,' narrated Mishra.

Murmu is fluent in Odia, Hindi and Santali, and her speeches in Santali are strongly worded and impactful, Mishra acknowledges. This makes her an excellent advocate for the tribal community and an ideal president of the nation.

THE BRAHMA KUMARIS AND WOMEN'S EMANCIPATION

Murmu's belief in God, her spiritual leaning and respect for all religions have always been an integral part of her. However, this hasn't remained a personal allegiance alone—it has translated into action. She has raised her voice for women's empowerment across the country in various capacities, and this has begun with her own struggles from the early years of her life as much as due to her association with the BKs.

The BKs from various parts of the country rejoiced at Murmu's elevation to the top position. Terming her life as 'difficult', the head of the organization in Rajasthan, Dadi Ratan Mohini, said that Murmu is the right candidate given her dedication and determination to change things, and her elevation to the post will bring about many changes, most importantly, women's empowerment.

Dadi Ratan Mohini said that it is matter of great

happiness that a person with 'outstanding thoughts, vision, routine, spiritual lifestyle and a noble character is the nation's head. This will strengthen women empowerment in the country'.[13]

'Without Shakti (woman), Shiva (man) is incomplete,' Murmu said while addressing a BK gathering in Jharkhand. 'Woman is a sign of power. The world is full of negativity because we neglect women. The need of the hour is getting women into all fields, even if it is through reservation in jobs, politics and any other field. Women have so much potential; it is time to explore that to make the world a better place,' she stated. 'Lead by example', she exhorted, adding that we all need to stress on being clean and pure from within than focussing on mere outward looks.[14]

She also said in one such meeting with BKs that 'women open the door to heaven and that is why all BK centres across the world have women leaders who preach and practice meditation to help face the challenges of life'. Addressing a meeting in Sonotel Garden in Dhanbad in 2017, she narrated in a nutshell why she chose to be a follower of the sect.[15]

Though it was not possible on her part to visit the Rairangpur BK ashram after she assumed the office of the governor of Jharkhand due to protocol, she has

---

[13]"Murmu Led Life of Difficulties, Her Elevation Will Strengthen Women Empowerment: Brahma Kumaris,' *The Print*, 21 July 2022, https://bit.ly/3IReePa. Accessed on 6 March 2023.

[14]"Woman Is the Doorway to Heaven,' YouTube, https://bit.ly/3lqqP4m. Accessed on 21 March 2023.

[15]'Draupadi Murmu Speech | Draupadi Murmu Addressing at Sonotel Garden | Brahma Kumaris Dhanbad | 2017,' YouTube, https://bit.ly/3LtmojH. Accessed on 16 March 2022.

continued her spiritual practices, including Raja Yoga, till date. However, she got more opportunities to reach out to many BK centres throughout the nation, where she went personally and addressed gatherings.

Women's empowerment is a recurring discourse in most of her speeches. She feels that slowly yet steadily, society has started looking at women in all fields with respect. If one woman sets an example, there will be many to emulate her. Women have been performing very well in every sphere of life like education, science, sports and politics. She said that Odisha has 50 per cent reservation for women in panchayati raj institutions.[16]

Years ago, Murmu used to say that one must have the passion to achieve something and never look down upon oneself:

> Everyone has the potential to perform, be it a man or a woman. For example, to run a family successfully, there is always the need for equal contribution of a man and woman. A country, too, needs both for growth and development. People say Santals are progressive, true, but there is need for more development. This is just the foundation stage and there is a long way to go.[17]

She asserted that whoever has the means to achieve something and reaches a height must always ensure that those below the average level are given a push. No wonder, in every step of her life, Murmu has tried to make way for more women to get into mainstream and become self-sufficient.

---

[16]Ibid.
[17]"Tejasvani: Guest Draupadi Murmu, Governor of Jharkhand,' YouTube, https://bit.ly/3kY7oQb. Accessed on 10 March 2023; author's paraphrase and translation.

Murmu visited Haryana and met Anganwadi workers and women sportspersons for an interaction in November 2022.[18] Apart from encouraging them in their pursuits and achievements, she gave an ear to all the women who narrated their stories of grit and determination in adverse conditions. Murmu was visibly moved listening to stories of female infanticide and the way Anganwadi workers broke the nexus of clinics determining the sex of the child in the womb, the middlemen and the families availing this service to stop this practice. 'Is this aversion to having girls only present in men or in women too? Do these would-be mothers also want to kill the daughters in the womb?' she asked. 'Women exist, and that is how men, too, come to the world. The roles both play are complementary,' is how she stated the importance of giving equal life to men and women. *'Beti bachao, beti padhao* is not an urban phenomenon; it is about every person in society being conscious about giving equal opportunity to women as much as men. So girls must be brought to this world and made self-sufficient,' she asserted.

In the national campaign called Rising India through Spiritual Empowerment (RISE) organized by the BKs that Murmu attended, her strong bonding with the sect was reaffirmed. Murmu began her address with gratitude to have the opportunity to speak at 'Indrasabha', meaning the place where gods meet. Considering herself as an invitee of the 'Almighty Baba', she spoke on spiritual empowerment to the large audience.[19]

---

[18]'President Droupadi Murmu Interacts with ASHA Workers, Women Sportspersons and Students in Chandigarh,' YouTube, https://bit.ly/3FFME6V. Accessed on 21 March 2023.
[19]'President Droupadi Murmu Launches the National Campaign on RISE

'*Samay se pehle, bhagya se zyada kuch nahi hone wala hai* [Nothing that is before time and more than destiny will happen],' she said. A golden India can be moulded with spiritual empowerment. 'I know how internal spirituality enlightened me when I was in a state of darkness and hopelessness. The BKs who are behind the conceptualization of RISE are the right people to take up such an important role in national development,' the President said. She added:

> It is a matter of pride that, in the last eighty years, the BKs have done a lot of work in the fields of personality development, service to mankind, uplifting the world through spiritual practices, inculcation of peace, holistic education, improvement of villages, empowering the poor and downtrodden, working during disasters, taking care of orphans, addressing environmental concerns and many more, which I may fall short to narrate.

The BKs is the biggest women-driven organization in the world and is active in 137 countries with more than 5,000 centres that serve people. In the organization, women are the heads. Murmu asserted that if the world can be led by women, it would be full of love, peace and happiness.

Addressing the nation on the eve of Republic Day, she raised the subject of women in nation-building.

> On [the] seventy-fourth Republic Day, we should remember the role of the jurist B.N. Rau, who had prepared the initial draft of the Constitution, and other experts and officers who helped in making of

---

Organized by Brahma Kumaris,' YouTube, http://bit.ly/42tsSFp. Accessed on 21 March 2023.

the Constitution. We are proud of the fact that the members of that assembly represented all regions and communities of India and that they included fifteen women too. India's Mars Mission was powered by a team of extraordinary women, and our sisters and daughters are not far behind in other areas either. Women's empowerment and gender equality are no longer mere slogans, as we have made great progress towards these ideals in recent years. With people's participation in Beti Bachao, Beti Padhao campaign, women's representation has been rising in every sphere of activity. During my visits to various states, educational institutions and while meeting delegations of various professionals, I have been amazed by the confidence of young women. I have no doubt in my mind that they are the ones who will do the most to shape tomorrow's India. What miracles cannot be achieved if this half of the population is encouraged to contribute to nation-building to the best of their ability?'[20]

In December 2022, Pragnya Reddy, the granddaughter-in-law of the owner of the popular sweet shop chain G. Pulla Reddy Sweets, wrote to Murmu seeking justice in a dowry harassment case. In her letter, she reportedly mentioned details of the harassment and even claimed that her in-laws were trying to kill her and her daughter. 'As the first citizen of India, and as a woman and a mother who experienced trials and tribulations in life, I am sure Your Excellency would understand my plight and leverage

---

[20] 'Address to the Nation by the Hon'ble President of India Smt. Droupadi Murmu on the Eve of the 74th Republic Day,' *Press Information Bureau*, 25 January 2023, https://bit.ly/3TGSD0T. Accessed on 21 March 2023.

this interaction to do justice to me,' she wrote. In response to the mail, the president, through her secretary, asked Andhra Pradesh's chief secretary to meet Pragnya and gather additional details about her grievance so that it could be redressed.[21]

This was not a one-off incident. Emphasizing her clarion call for women's emancipation, Murmu, while addressing the probationers of the seventy-fourth batch of the Indian Police Service at the Sardar Vallabhbhai Patel National Police Academy, said that 'Atmanirbhar Bharat' pre-supposes 'Atmanirbhar Nari' [self-reliant woman]. She asserted that 'Nari Shakti' has to play a major role in achieving India's own targets during Amrit Kaal and stressed on the inclusion of women in ensuring sustainable development. 'Inclusion means inclusion of the last person, the most deprived person, the most vulnerable person. That person should be at the centre of the police officers' concerns,' she said. As always, she advised the probationers to be sensitive to the plight of the voiceless. 'We should quickly move on from the phase of empowering women to the stage of women-led development. It is already happening in many fields; it must happen in a bigger way,' she exhorted.[22]

Many times, she has become emotional talking about female infanticide. At one instance, she said:

> Girls give and spread love. People who kill them in the womb are not aware that they are killing devis

---

[21] 'President Droupadi Murmu Directs AP Chief Secretary to Meet Dowry Victim Pragnya,' *The New Indian Express*, 29 December 2022, https://bit.ly/3knokz7. Accessed on 23 February 2023.
[22] 'President Droupadi Murmu Addresses the Officer Trainees of Indian Police Service (74th RR Batch),' YouTube, http://bit.ly/3JUi6k9. Accessed on 21 March 2023.

and lakshmis. Girls are Shakti *swaroopa* [incarnation of power]. Look at how our sportswomen have fared—they have made us proud. Women and men should walk hand in hand for the growth of the nation. We need to support women because in our country, the social structures have ignored them for years. Now is the time for the renaissance moment.[23]

Earlier, during her term in Odisha, she would always give examples of women leaders from Odisha as well as the rest of India who have had important roles in the freedom struggle and nation-building. Former CM of Odisha Nandini Satpathy, freedom fighter Sarojini Naidu and many others were regular references in her deliberations as her inspiration. She would also talk about the circumstances that made or marred women leaders. Murmu felt:

> Some women leaders earlier belonged to influential families and they had the support of many people around them, but for those like me, the journey at every step was thorny. In the beginning, women in politics were only considered respectful if they had a lineage of politics in the family. But whatever support I have had was from people in the party who stood by me since the day I stepped into politics, and they continue to do so even today. I could also survive in politics because my constituents love me.[24]

---

[23] 'President Droupadi Murmu Interacts with ASHA Workers, Women Sportspersons and Students in Chandigarh,' YouTube, https://bit.ly/3FFME6V. Accessed on 21 March 2023.
[24] 'An Exclusive Interview with India's First Tribal President, Draupadi Murmu by Dr. Itirani Samanta,' YouTube, http://bit.ly/420iZ1w. Accessed on 10 March 2023.

Murmu believes that while it has become easy for women these days to do something they want, the world continues to be male-dominated. 'To bring about change, it is important to have a reservation policy for women in every field because men have dominated all fields for a very long time. Ticket distribution for women in the political parties is still tricky. Giving women an equal footing with men could add a lot of value to the world at large.'

In the Global Gender Gap Report 2022 brought out by the World Economic Forum, India's ranking in the international gender index has remained close to the bottom—a dismal 135 out of 140 countries in 2022, and 140 out of 156 in 2021. Worse still, India has made little progress on any of the four important parameters determining the rankings. Amending the electoral laws or the Constitution of India to reserve one-third of the legislature and parliamentary seats for women has not been implemented in letter or spirit. In the run-up to elections, politicians make promises to support such legislation, but they are in vain. Ever since the reservation of seats for women at the panchayat and municipal levels has been initiated, a perceptible change in the priorities and programme implementation of most such democratic institutions has been seen, and most women leaders feel such prioritization should be done vigorously and regularly.

A WARRIOR FOR THE DOWNTRODDEN

President Murmu's appeals have not been restricted to women. She is a warrior for all the downtrodden, constantly fighting to improve the lives of the people, which has been a mantra for her even before she began public service.

The president's words are not only from her extensive reading but practical experience that comes out as mantras of existence for others. On 27 November 2022, on the occasion of Constitution Day, when Murmu addressed a gathering of Cabinet ministers, justices and chief justices, her words resonated across the nation. The video released by the President of India handle on YouTube went viral within minutes of Murmu's touching presentation of a sensitive issue. Subtly yet sternly, she expressed her dissatisfaction with the judiciary. She let them know what is desired of the lawyers and judges to provide justice quickly, particularly to the poor and vulnerable. She said:

> I grew up in a small village that had no basic facilities. We used to consider three kinds of professionals—teachers, doctors and lawyers—as gods. Teachers teach us, doctors save our lives and lawyers bail us out of trouble. The trouble could be as little trouble as slapping someone or as large as killing. As an MLA, I was leading a home standing committee in Odisha and wanted to visit jails across the state. It was not imposed on me but I wanted to find out how people live in the jail, what food they eat, what the facilities and conditions are like and what led the prisoners to be bound in jail. I was appalled by the situation in jails and more so with the reason some of them were stuck inside.[25]

Some prisoners had spent twenty-five years and more in the jail. They do not know when their ordeal will be over and when they can come out.

---

[25] 'President Murmu's Valedictory Address at Constitution Day Celebrations Organised by Supreme Court,' YouTube, http://bit.ly/3LGq0yQ. Accessed on 21 March 2023.

She had submitted the report to the director general of police and asked him to discuss the reform recommendations with the CM. This, she believed, could help prisoners languishing in jail for years.

Remembering her tenure in Jharkhand, where she had taken revolutionary measures to close cases that ran for years, she told the judges:

> I was aghast to find teachers absent from classes across the state as most of them were attending to minor cases in the hundreds. I sought the intervention of the judiciary, and I had opportunity to meet justices of the Jharkhand High Court. Bose ji and Birender ji, who officiated my oath-taking ceremony, were the ones I discussed the issue with. But two more justices, P.K. Mohanty and D.N. Patel, need a special mention for taking my ideas forward. [...] It so happened that I called Justice P.K. Mohanty ji and sought his help in disposing of the cases. Around 5,000 cases were resolved in a day and the second time too in the higher education department, many others were disposed of.

Her concern for those in prison was coming from the heart. Speaking of the people in the jails, she said that they do not know about their fundamental rights, preamble or even fundamental duty. She said:

> Just because someone slapped someone in the influence of addictive drinks and food, which is common in the backward states and communities, they were booked under many sections of the IPC, and some sections were inappropriately tagged. Their families, too, do not have the capacity to bail them out as they fear they

would have to part with whatever little they have—land or property—in paying the legal fees for the trials. The prisoners are also not interested in coming out after years of captivity due to the stigma attached in our society.

She expressed her desire for the legal system to help bail these prisoners out of further years in jail and more trouble. The more the jails are overcrowded, the greater is the burden on the government. She stated:

> We should think about human rights and also how we can upskill [the prisoners] to make them self-sufficient. Instead we keep them confined, while many people who actually commit crimes are roaming scot-free. Legislature, executive and judiciary are three major wings of democracy. We are by the people, of the people and for the people, so let us think and act together. We do not need more prisons if we call ourselves developing or progressing. *Yeh kaisa vikas hai* (What kind of development is this)? We should think of a way to lessen the number of prisons.

To the judges present, Murmu left her speech open-ended: 'I have delivered half of the speech I wanted to; whatever I left unsaid is up to you all to understand and act.' That must have left the legal luminaries thinking.

Referring to this deliberation, BJP leader Surama Padhy reminisced her days with Murmu when both were active in state politics as legislators—Murmu in Rairangpur, Mayurbhanj district and Padhy in Ranpur, Nayagarh district. She explained that even back then, Murmu used to be candid and to the point. She was known as an efficient legislator because of her ability to comprehend and speak her mind and be straightforward. She also cited Murmu's meticulousness in working for all the house committees she was heading in the state. 'Her recommendations were weighty and such that the government was left with no option but to act because she was thorough with the laws, rights and privileges under the Constitution,' Padhy stressed.

Apart from her sympathy for and work with prisoners, Murmu's concern for and connect with children, too, are discerningly evident. The extensive work she did in transforming the education system in Jharkhand is a testament to this, and her tilt towards the cause has remained the same even after her election as president. Meeting school children on Children's Day in 2022, she spoke on how to beat odds with a hope for a better tomorrow. She spoke about the kuchha floors of her classrooms when she was in the school and how the students used to sit on potato sacks instead of chairs and tables. At the Rashtrapati Bhavan, Murmu told the children:

> I was full of hope when I was a kid. I would be happy thinking that if I am in this classroom today, I will be in the next classroom tomorrow. If this year, I have one frock, the next year, I may have two. Be positive that things will change. But I do not want you to follow anyone. Carve a path of your own and have an identity that will remain unparalleled.[26]

---

[26] 'President Murmu Assumed the Role of an Affable Teacher and Guide to Students on Children's Day,' YouTube, http://bit.ly/3n7B266. Accessed on 21 March 2023.

MOTHER, MOTHERLAND AND MOTHER TONGUE

Not only has Murmu made efforts to give tribal people their due, she has been pushing for investment in education in one's mother tongue, which may bring more and more people to learning and training institutions. Addressing the convocation of Doon University on 9 December 2022, Murmu spoke about how being educated could make a world of difference and giving importance to mother tongues can prove to be a blessing.

> Today, India is being looked at by the world in awe. India is a sign of *vasudhaiva kutumbakam*. Our unity in diversity is an example for many and we must be educated to lead the country forward. *Matrubhumi, matrubhasa aur maa* [motherland, mother tongue and mother] all are equally important. Learning *kitabi bhasa* [bookish language] is fine as long as writing exam papers is concerned but do not forget your roots—your mother tongue, your own language. *Maa jaisi hoti hai, achhi hoti hai... Matrubhasa logon ke nazar mein jaisa bhi ho, apna hota hai* [Mother is always the embodiment of good; similarly, mother tongue is one's own and the best]. Do your duty for the motherland, love your mother and speak your mother tongue.[27]

Her concern for children in tribal-dominated areas, their education and need to use their mother tongue in education is understandable given the Bharat Rural Livelihoods Foundation Report published in 2022. The

---

[27]'President Droupadi Murmu Graces the 3rd Convocation of Doon University at Dehradun,' YouTube, https://bit.ly/40iCSj2. Accessed on 21 March 2023.

survey was conducted in Schedule V areas (states which have significant ST population)—Andhra Pradesh (including Telangana), Jharkhand, Chhattisgarh, Himachal Pradesh, Madhya Pradesh, Gujarat, Odisha and Rajasthan. It pointed out that the dropout rates, especially in elementary classes in tribal areas of Chhattisgarh, Jharkhand, Madhya Pradesh, Rajasthan and Odisha, are much higher than in other communities.

There could be many factors behind this trend, the first being not using the mother tongue as a medium of instruction in primary classes in tribal areas. In most tribal-dominated areas, the dialect is different and affects education at the primary level. However, the New Education Policy (NEP), 2020, advocating use of 'home language' in foundation classes is expected to address this issue.

Murmu stated that even during her schooling in the 1970s, the teachers were from other districts and towns. This was a problem because the gap in understanding due to a language barrier between the teachers and students was wide. This problem continues today as well—difference in language creates a vacuum of understanding and becomes a problem for children. Teachers from other places hardly know the native language. The issue is more concerning among the STs in comparison to other communities. It is for this reason that the need for a script for Santals was also felt and approved.

In a step towards mother tongue-based teaching, Murmu released technical books of the All India Council for Technical Education in Odia language in Bhubaneswar during her visit. She said, 'Learning in their mother tongue will help develop creative thinking and analytical skills among children of all age groups and provide equal opportunities to students in both urban and rural areas.'[28]

She expressed her appreciation for the importance the NEP gives to all Indian languages and said that the policy will help learning and teaching and go a long way in ensuring education for the masses. To help students understand technical education in English, the NEP, 2020, envisages technical education in regional languages.

'Research has shown that intellectual development of children learning in their mother tongue is greater compared to those learning in other languages. In fact, a student entering the school for the first time feels much more comfortable if interacted with in their mother tongue. As a result, the process of schooling becomes easier for the child,' she said.

'Since culture and mother tongue are interconnected, a student learns much more and becomes aware of their culture and heritage,' Murmu further stated. She emphasized the importance of education as a tool for empowerment and exhorted that each and every child in the country should have access to education at every level.

Stressing on Odia as an ancient language, Murmu said that it has a rich and distinct literary tradition and vocabulary. It has also received the distinction of a classical language. Most Indian languages have more or less the same potential. Much before taking over as the president, she addressed a gathering, stating, '*Aau jete bhasa parucha sikha nija matrubhasa ra mahata rakha* [Learn as many languages as you can but mother tongue should remain

---

[28]'Learning in Mother Tongue Helps Build a Vibrant Society: President', *The New Indian Express*, 11 November 2022, https://bit.ly/3ZGOo7d. Accessed on 6 March 2023.

the most important].[29] Thus, her concern about the mother tongue is not recent; she has always been linked to the grassroots and has a clear understanding of how important it is to learn in one's mother tongue.

Always a proud Odia, Murmu has spoken endlessly about Odisha during her gubernatorial stint in Jharkhand. Odisha is a *shastriya bhumi* (classical land) and its language, dance, music are also classical. 'Among world languages, Odia stands in the thirty-seventh position, and in Indian languages, it is in the tenth position.' Murmu asserted that Odia is considered the best Aryan language and should not be considered as a regional language. She added that among the Dravidian languages that have been granted classical status are Telugu, Tamil, Malayalam and Kannada.

Similarly, throwing light on the folk tradition of Odisha, Murmu cited the rich repository of folk, martial and classical dances like Chhau, Gotipua, Dalkhai and Jhumar, which are all unique and enjoyed by the masses. She said:

> Our Adivasi music and rhythm are matchless. Our filigree, Pipili appliqué and handloom works are much sought after worldwide. We have the legacy of artistes like Jitendriya Haripal, Upendra Bhanja, Fakir Mohan, Utkalamani Gopabandhu, Harekrushna Mahatab, Jayee Rajguru, Buxi Jagabandhu and Baji Rout, who have done the state proud. We also have women leaders like Maa Rama Devi, Sarala Devi, Malati Choudhury and Prabati Giri, who are inspiration for generations to come.[30]

---

[29]'Droupadi Murmu, Governor of Jharkhand | Ama Utkarsha Odisha @ Mumbai,' YouTube, https://bit.ly/3FGSNQ7. Accessed on 21 March 2023.
[30]Ibid.

Rath Yatra is a world event now and Odisha's food is relished around the globe.

She also stressed sticking to the mother tongue when people from the same state meet each other by stating, 'I urge all Odias to speak in Odia whenever they meet anyone from Odisha. We must stand out as Odias. Jagannath culture is all about simplicity without any ill feeling for anyone. Let us all symbolize Odia culture and keep the flag of Odisha high. The same applies to people from other states as well.'

A PRESIDENTIAL VISIT HOME

Surama Padhy met Murmu when she visited Odisha on 10 November 2022. 'It was late and her security people were restricting everyone from entering the meeting chamber when Didi saw me. She asked them to let me in. Her personal equations with people are a notch above everything else and cannot be bound by protocol,' said Padhy.

On landing in Bhubaneswar for her maiden visit after becoming the president, she was accorded a grand welcome by the governor Professor Ganeshi Lal, CM Naveen Patnaik and the Union minister Dharmendra Pradhan at the Biju Patnaik International Airport in Bhubaneswar. She, then, left for Puri for the *darshan* [glimpse of a deity] of the Trinity in Srimandir. However, on reaching Puri Grand Road, Madam President decided to walk till the temple gates without caring for official protocol.

The crowd that had gathered on Grand Road was excited to see the president up close, and Murmu waved at some while making salutation to others. She also went close to the children in school uniform and shook hands with some. As a teacher, years ago, she loved to give chocolates to her students, and she did the same in Puri when she saw children lined up. She asked her staff to distribute chocolates among them. Before entering the temple, she touched the Aruna Stambha, the pillar at the entrance of the temple and bowed down, touching the soil with her head to offer prayers.

Like every Odia, Murmu's association with Lord Jagannath is long and strong. As described previously, she made sure to ask a friend to offer prayers at His feet before she left for Delhi, since she didn't have the time to do so herself. Her knowledge about Jagannath *sanskruti*—the cultural heritage associated with Lord Jagannath—is vast and she considers it as the guiding force of all Odias.

At one of the events she attended in Mumbai while she was the Jharkhand governor, Murmu spoke extensively on ahimsa as religion, Jagannath culture and how Odisha represents it. 'Sri Jagannath is close to everyone's heart. He is the symbol of Odisha's life and culture. Odisha is synonymous to Jagannath and vice-versa. When Anantavarman Chodaganga started constructing the Jagannath temple in the eleventh century, it became the life centre of all Hindus,' she said.[31]

A staunch follower of the Jagannath tradition, she feels the culture of Lord Jagannath has spread far and wide, encouraging humility and tolerance in humanity. 'It is He who teaches us to be caring for others, He is above any caste or creed and language,' she said.[32] The same

---
[31]Ibid.
[32]Ibid.

emotions were also echoed by her daughter, who said that her mother is a follower of the Jagannath sanskruti. Murmu stated:

> In Adivasi culture, we worship forests and woods, we worship '*daru* brahma' (Lord Jagannath). Lord Jagannath's idol is made of daru [wood]. As Hindus, we worship Vishnu *pratima* [statue]; the core is the same. In the Jagannath temple, people partake of *mahaprasad* (offering of food to Jagannath) together. The Lord doesn't differentiate between caste and creed. The religion of humanity prevails in Jagannath culture, nothing else. We must take it forward.[33]

As India nears 100 years of freedom and is making a mark in every sphere in the world, it is the responsibility of every Indian to be an example to spread the message of shanti and ahimsa that the country is known for through the teachings of the father of the nation, Mahatma Gandhi.

Murmu added that Gandhi was the flag bearer of ahimsa. It is through his leadership through ahimsa that India got independence. This goes on to prove that it is by means of ahimsa that we can also achieve peace, in the twenty-first century. At Puri Srimandir, a servitor who served the president said, 'Madam Murmu was happy yet calm while taking darshan of the deities inside the *Garbha Gruha* [sanctum sanctorum]. She prayed for the well-being of the people as well as progress and prosperity of our nation. She offered prayers for around fifteen minutes.'[34]

---

[33]Ibid.
[34]'President Droupadi Murmu at Puri Jagannath Temple, Writes about Her Srimandir Experience,' YouTube, https://bit.ly/3lyy75U. Accessed on 23 March 2023.

Murmu also wrote the same in the visitor's register in her own handwriting and signed it. After returning from Puri, Murmu attended a felicitation ceremony organized by the Odisha government at the Raj Bhavan. Speaking to the audience there, Murmu spoke about her feeling for the country and the state she was born in. 'Our country is gold; its water, life and every characteristic has inspired me. Being a daughter of the country has been too gratifying,' she said. Narrating the contribution of Odia freedom fighters, she spoke about Paika Bidroha [Paika Rebellion] in 1817 and the efforts of Buxi Jagabandhu and Jayee Rajguru in it. She also hailed Utkalamani Gopabandhu Das and Utkal Gourab Madhusudan Das for their valour during the freedom struggle. 'Gandhi ji spoke in praise of women freedom fighters from Odisha like Maa Rama Devi, Sarala Devi and Malati Devi for their courage,' she stressed. On Odisha's potential to become one of the most prosperous states in the country, Murmu spoke at length about its human resource, which she said is rich scientifically and culturally, and its vast natural resources.

On the second day of her visit to Odisha, as she went to the Tapovan High School, where she was a frequent visitor as a point of reference for students wishing to get admissions to the school, Murmu got emotional. She spoke to a group of students and ex-students and explained the struggles she had faced in Uparbeda.

> I had no knowledge of the world outside Uparbeda, my native place. I studied whatever was in the school curriculum, but beyond that, I was clueless about everything else. My grandmother was my inspiration. [...] My paternal grandmother was revered by

everyone in the village because of her knowledge. She inspired me to go for higher studies, just not at the cost of household work. She wanted girls to be experts in everything. Even in matters concerning the health of village women, my grandmother would find solutions.[35]

Speaking about the dearth of facilities back in the 1970s, she exhorted the students to take advantage of the present-day education system. 'I urge you all to learn at the schools but not forget to give back to the school, the state and the country something in return by way of knowledge and expertise. Contribute to the world around you to make it a better place to live in,' said Murmu, encouraging the students.

Later, she reached the Government Girls High School to address a gathering and met her batchmates who she had earlier asked to be present so that they could have a meeting with her after forty-eight years, although some of them were already in touch with her.

'Where is Chunni?' she asked as soon as she saw her group of friends. On hearing that President Murmu had asked about her, Chunni, that is, Chinmayee Gochchayat was filled with joy. 'I could not believe that Murmu looked for me during her visit. I was away in Puttaparthi, but I got to know about her request when media houses started calling me up to find my relation with her. It was then that I realized how much importance she laid on friendship and remembered me,' she said.

---

[35]'Governor Ganeshi Lal, Dharmendra Pradhan and President Murmu Visit Tapoban High School,' YouTube, https://bit.ly/3yXJEPu. Accessed on 21 March 2023.

After watching the media reports, Chinmayee was happy to see that President Murmu had worn an Odisha handloom sari that she and her sister Tanmayee had gifted her. Both the sisters and their families had been to Rashtrapati Bhavan to meet Her Excellency after she was sworn in. 'A sari is a small token of appreciation and love from school friends but she made its worth much more by wearing it,' said an elated Chinmayee. After school and college life, while Murmu was busy in her job and family, Chinmayee, too, had gotten married to a doctor and settled down after getting a job as a teacher. Their telephonic conversations began only after Murmu became a minister in the Odisha government and they continue to remain in touch till date.

Similarly, Dangi Murmu, who was present at the Government Girls High School, Unit 2, which the president visited and addressed the students, was at a loss for words. After their school days, she had reconnected with Murmu during her ministerial term in the BJD–BJP alliance government in Odisha in her quarters. Moved to tears, Dangi said:

> She does not seem to have changed, even with so many achievements. Her characteristic traits were exactly as you see today. She has evolved in politics and governance. She is so well read now that she talks impromptu on subjects beyond the understanding of common people. Murmu is an example of an ideal woman who has struggled to the top position of the country.

She recollected Murmu's personal losses and said that with so many trials and tribulations, only Murmu could stand unmoved in difficult times and still work for the people. 'Tremendous willpower and dedication to the service of the nation has taken her to the position. It's absolutely her hard work that paid off,' added Dangi, who was one of the chosen few of Murmu's friends to have participated in her swearing-in ceremony at the Rashtrapati Bhavan. She stated:

> We have not been able to give her anything, but Murmu has given all of her friends so much respect and adoration. It would never have been possible for all of us to step into the Rashtrapati Bhavan otherwise. The reception we got, the prestige we were accorded as the president's friends, the treatment meted out to us are prized for us. We had never seen something so ceremonial and regal like what we saw at the Rashtrapati Bhavan.

Dangi added that it is now up to Murmu to keep in touch with them amid her busy schedule, as they cannot reach her directly while she is in office. 'We cannot call her at will or talk to her or meet her. She has to keep the loop going if she wishes to as she is in the highest constitutional post,' said Dangi. Murmu met around ten to twelve of her close school friends at the function.

LOOKING TO THE FUTURE

Given the Constitutional provisions, how much of a proactive role Murmu will be able to play and pursue an agenda of action as the president remains to be seen in the next four years. In almost all matters of state, the president is required to go by the recommendations of the Council of Ministers and does not have much discretion. Having said that, it is worth recalling the power of withholding assent to bills approved by Parliament that Murmu, as the governor of Jharkhand, wilfully exercised in the greater interest of the tribals. There is precedent of presidents having expressed reservations on certain legislative proposals on grounds of them not representing the wider public interest.

Someone who has maintained Constitutional checks and balances as a governor is unlikely to buckle under pressure in the most important position. Particularly when it comes to tribal rights and welfare, her affinity to the community will also be a major factor. Concerns regarding tribal rights have seen a rise in India for quite some time now. Unrest has also been seen in tribal majority states, and successive state governments have not been as successful in dealing with these issues.

Former assistant professor at Fakir Mohan College Balasore, Indira Dutta, who knew Murmu personally while she was posted in Maharaja Purna Chandra Autonomous College, Baripada, and Government Women's College, Baripada, felt that her political leaning notwithstanding, Murmu, expectedly, will exercise thoughtfulness and Constitutional propriety in pushing forward her concerns on issues she feels strongly about, particularly relating to the tribals.[36] She will ensure that the country's outlook towards the tribal communities and concerns certainly get attention. Moreover, she felt that she will get the support of the BJP in promoting the welfare of the Adivasis, for which the groundwork was laid by selecting an Adivasi as the president.

---

[36] All quotes by Indira Dutta are from an interview conducted by the author on 16 December 2022.

Dutta believed that with Murmu's vehemence in standing firm during the passing of Bills pertaining to the Santals' land rights during her term as the governor, Murmu comes across as a person who has a deep understanding of tribal identity. She said that Murmu was the best person to protect the Adivasis. She had done it in the past by refusing to accept the Bills that went against the legitimate rights of the tribals and this stand was likely to further strengthen, given her conviction to the cause.

Dutta also stated that there is a stark need for course correction in matters concerning the tribals, who have been living in abject neglect for ages now. She stated that giving them the life all others live in this country and bringing them out of isolation by educating them is of prime importance for the powers that be and if Murmu fulfils this, her term will be considered the golden era of India's presidentship.

On meeting Murmu recently, after she became the president, Morada MLA Rajkishore Das, a member of the BJD, said that she is likely to make a lot of revolutionary changes as she has always wanted to, even as a minister. 'She has not changed a bit. She has also changed the concept of political opponent,' said Das. On seeing him from a distance at the governor's house in Bhubaneswar, Murmu called Das in and spoke to him for a few minutes without adhering to protocol.

'Now I am in BJD; that way, I am a political opponent of the BJP. But being on a Constitutional post, she really does not care as far as personal relationships are concerned. We have close family relations,' explained an emotional Das. He continued:

When I was denied a ticket from the BJP in the last general elections and decided to fight from the BJD, I got to know that she did not want me to leave the BJP. She is believed to have spoken to party members that I need to stay in the party for the betterment of people of Mayurbhanj in general and Rairangpur in particular. That speaks volumes about her integrity, dignity and clean conscience.

'*Mo jibana dhanya hei gala* [Murmu's presidentship has made my life worthwhile]' was how Das expressed his feelings on her becoming the president of the country. This was because many believe that Das gave Murmu her first opportunity, when she contested the NAC elections way back in 1997.

Bir Singh Munda, secretary of Adivasi National Convention Committee in Jharkhand, hoped that their demands to give all Adivasis ST status will be granted by Murmu as the Constitutional head. Similarly, tribes from different parts expressed happiness, since someone from their community was elevated to the topmost seat and will hear them out when there will be a need.

Leading the Adivasi Sengel Abhiyan Tribal Empowerment Campaign, Salkhan Murmu said that Adivasis have been exploited for a long time, but with Murmu as the president, some changes for the betterment of tribals are certainly expected. 'As governor of Jharkhand, Murmu had shown grit in negating an attempt by a previous BJP government led by Raghubar Das in matters of two Acts. We are sure she will stand by tribals,' he said.

'President Droupadi Murmu will prove to be the voice of the Adivasi community and an ambassador of Jharkhand's Santali culture,' said Raghubar Das during a celebration of Murmu's historic election as the fifteenth president of India by members of Sampoorna Adivasi Samaj at Jehra, Tola Basti, Baridih.[37]

On 5 September 2022, President Murmu bestowed teachers across the country with national awards. Around forty-six teachers from different states went to the Rashtrapati Bhavan to accept the honour. Murmu, in her speech, dedicated her achievement to her teachers, without whose contribution she wouldn't have been the first girl to have stepped out of confines of the village to be educated. 'They have held my hands and taught me to fight the world's challenges. That is why today I have been able to break barriers and glass ceilings at many places,' she said.

Her rootedness as an Adivasi to jal, jungle aur jameen was reflected in her address to the Indian Forest Service officers at a function.[38]

> I remember when I was a kid, we used to cook with wood. But every time my father went to get wood from trees, he would pray and then cut the logs. Once I asked him why and what he prayed for. And I was told that he prays to the tree for forgiveness before cutting it. 'Just because of our requirement to cook, we are forced to fell trees. I seek forgiveness from the tree and nature,' my father had explained. I realized later that even before ploughing the land, we pray

---

[37]'Droupadi Murmu to Become Voice of Adivasi Community: Raghubar Das,' *The Avenue Mail*, 21 July 2022, http://bit.ly/3lEEzbz. Accessed on 21 March 2023.
[38]'President Droupadi Murmu Addresses Probationers of Indian Forest Service,' YouTube, https://bit.ly/40oCbV3. Accessed on 21 March 2023.

to Mother Earth for giving her pain. But that is how we cultivate crops. Mother Earth, trees and forests, which give us food to eat, need to be nurtured and taken care of.

Months into her presidential tenure, not much has changed in Uparbeda. In the village, the lone health and wellness centre that is meant for the hundreds of people from the seven peripheral villages has no manpower. Just one pharmacy staffer continues to treat people at the centre. In case of any medical requirement, most people visit the sub-divisional hospitals at Rairangpur and Karanjia, which are 15 km and 30 km, respectively, from the area. Villagers have pinned hope for a change soon if Murmu visits Uparbeda.

Naba Majhi, the Rairangpur MLA, believed that things will certainly change for the Adivasis and STs, as Murmu is at helm now. Personally, and for the people of the district, he expects her to take up the issue of railway connectivity to Badampahad. 'Currently, connectivity is there till Baripada and Bangiriposi on one side and Keonjhar on the other. Between them, there is no rail connectivity. It is high time that all parts of the district are connected via railway as that would benefit the lives and livelihoods of the people here. It would provide livelihood options to people too,' he said.

She gave a clarion call to the students during one of her interactions, asking each one of them to visit backward villages and feel the pulse. She asked them to look at how villagers live and check whether policies and schemes made are of help to the public. She urged them to interact with women and children and put their issues forward to the collector or district administration.

Since she assumed office as the president, people from her home state have been taking their demands to her in novel ways, expecting a solution. Four youths from Baripada in January set out on a *padayatra* [walk on foot] to New Delhi to meet President Murmu and apprise her of the issues faced by them. The four, including founder of Mayurbhanj Adivasi Students Association Suklal Marandi, Sauna Murmu, Badal Marandi and Laxmikanta Baskey, said that the tribal-dominated Mayurbhanj district is in the grip of problems like lack of jobs, health facilities, education, communication etc. 'The Sareikela–Kharsawan district, which was a part of Mayurbhanj and is now in Jharkhand, has been reeling under neglect in every sector of development due to the alleged apathy of the government there. Housing benefits under the government schemes do not reach the beneficiaries,' they added.[39]

The Mayurbhanj unit of the BJD expects the president to heed their demand to include Ho, Mundari and Bhumija scripts in the Eighth Schedule of the Constitution of India. Tribal leaders Sananda Marandi, Debasish Marandi and Bhadev Hansdah hope for the president's intervention into the matter. Besides Koraput unit of the BJD, too, has demanded ST status for 160 communities residing in the state. All these people are hopeful about being heard by Murmu.

While speaking at the seventeenth Pravasi Bharatiya Divas on 10 January 2023, President Murmu expressed her hope that the power of the diaspora will help inclusive

---

[39]'Padyatra by Four Tribals to Meet President Murmu,' *The New Indian Express*, 4 January 2023, https://bit.ly/3ZohV59. Accessed on 29 March 2023.

development of the nation. She asserted that it has become an important force and tremendous energy and confidence to infuse all those into the country'.

'Call of the motherland transcends barriers of time and distance. Despite their success in their adopted homes in different corners of the world, they would always hold a special place in our hearts as responsible stakeholders in India's development,' the president said.[40]

President Murmu has a clear vision for the future of India. On her hopes for a rising India, during the Pravasi Diwas, she expressed her desire to see the country leading world peace and developing science and spirituality in 2047, marking a 100 years of Indian Independence. 'I look forward to India becoming a knowledge superpower, full of sustainable development, with a prosperous society, where women are at equal footing with men and the marginalized on par with all others; all this will lead to world peace,' Murmu said.[41]

Citing the example of the pandemic era, she pointed at India's leading role in mitigating problems of other countries through supplying vaccines and medicines. Today, India is the fifth largest economy in the world and a G20 leader, proving that *vasudhaiva kutumbakam* continues to be our guiding principle.

President Murmu has been called a common person's president. Sensitivity to issues concerning every common person clearly comes up in every meeting she holds and every gathering she addresses. The common concerns of

---

[40] 'President Murmu Graces the Valedictory Session of the 17th Pravasi Bharatiya Divas Convention,' YouTube, https://bit.ly/3JXmq1Y. Accessed on 21 March 2023.
[41] Ibid.

community, caste, environment, forests, trees, health, education and children have been identified, addressed and validated in her speeches. Her emphasis on prioritizing nation and state, mother and mother tongue and community and its concerns touches the hearts of people from all parts of the country.

Patriotism underlies all her statements. However, it is not a recent phenomenon. Rather, she has always spoken about her feelings for the country as a proud Indian. While addressing the nation on the eve of Republic Day on 25 January 2023, she said:

> The respect that India has earned on the world stage has resulted in new opportunities as well as responsibilities. India holds the Group of 20 (G20) presidency this year, which is an opportunity to promote democracy and multilateralism and the right forum for shaping a better world and a better future. We have to look at the ancient traditions with a new perspective. We need to reconsider our basic priorities. The scientific aspects of traditional life-values have to be understood. We must, once again, rekindle that respect for nature and humility before the vast universe.[42]

'Live for others. Live and look behind and see how many are left behind and why. The "why" will answer all questions about problems people face,' Murmu said to the students of Padmavati University when she visited it

---

[42]'G20 Ideal Platform to Discuss Global Warming, Climate Change, Says Murmu,' *Business Standard*, 25 January 2023, https://bit.ly/3lAfheJ. Accessed on 23 March 2023.

on 5 December 2022.[43] 'Only when you live for others, your life will be worthwhile. But for that take others along in the journey like in case of self-help groups—*Ek akela thak jayega, mil kar bojh uthana* [Let us all unitedly lift the burden, lest we get tired alone],' she asserted, adding that education must be taken not as a quality but only a qualification.

> *Praninka arata dukha apramita, dekhu dekhu ke ba sahu,*
> *Mo jibana pache narke padhithau jagata uddhara hau*
> [Who can withstand the miseries and sufferings of the countless around,
> Let my life be in hell, let the world be redeemed.][44]

These lines of Odia poet Bhima Bhoi inscribed on the walls of the United Nations (UN) Hall echo the life motto of Murmu. She had concluded her maiden speech as the president with these lines.[45] Her exemplary service to mankind irrespective of the struggles and pains she has faced make her an indomitable and invincible people's president.

On 31 January 2023, President Murmu addressed the joint session in Parliament for the first time, asking every citizen of the country to perform their duties to the utmost. '"Amrit Kaal" of 25 years is the period of the golden centenary of independence and the making of a developed India. This 25-year span is an opportunity to build an

---

[43] 'President Murmu Interacts with Students and Women Achievers at Sri Padmavathi Women's University,' YouTube, https://bit.ly/3yXAvX6. Accessed on 21 March 2023.
[44] Translation by Dr Prasant Kumar Pradhan
[45] 'Full Text of Draupadi Murmu's Maiden Speech as President,' *OneIndia*, 25 July 2022, http://bit.ly/40o7rnl. Accessed on 21 March 2023.

era for which we need to work continuously with our full potential,' she said.[46]

She stressed on building a Bharat that is self-reliant, has no poverty, whose youth and women power are at the forefront to give direction to the society and the nation, whose diversity is even more vivid and whose unity becomes even more unshakeable.

'In almost nine years of my government's term, the [...] biggest change is that today every Indian's confidence is at its peak and the world's outlook towards India has changed. India, which once looked at others for solutions to most of its problems, is today emerging as a provider of solutions for the issues faced by the world,' she said.

Appreciating India's elevated position as the fifth largest economy in the world, Murmu said that India's commitment to public welfare, removing every obstacle being faced by women, protection of nature, preserving heritage and donning the rightful role on the global stage is praiseworthy. She stated with a sense of pride:

> This year, India has assumed the Presidency of an influential global group like G-20. With the mantra of One Earth, One Family, One Future, India is attempting to find collective solutions to the current global challenges in collaboration with the G-20 member countries. [...] We are chairing the SCO [Shanghai Cooperation Organisation] this year, and [...] being a member of the Quad, we are working for peace, stability and prosperity in the Indo-Pacific.

---

[46] 'President Murmu Addresses Joint Session in Parliament: Read Full Speech Here,' *Hindustan Times*, 31 January 2023, http://bit.ly/40kZlf4. Accessed on 21 March 2023.

She concluded her address by reciting a line from the Rig Veda:

Samgacchadhvam samvadadhvam sam vo manaamsi jaanataam.
[Let us walk together step by step, understand each other's mind and let there be a flow of unity in our resolutions.]

Acknowledgements

I am thankful to *The New Indian Express* and my colleagues to have supported me in undertaking the work. My gratitude also goes out to Maa, who always boosted my morale with her one-liner, 'You are the best', and Jagi, who made that special call to me on Durgashtami of 2022. Thanks to Yamini for trusting me, to Aurodeep for working with the manuscript meticulously and to Smita for those questions that otherwise would have remained unanswered.

A word of gratitude also goes to Sukant Sahu and Subrat Sahu, who made my tour to the nooks and crannies of Mayurbhanj district easy and seamless.

I am thankful to my daughter Gudia and husband Titoo for being my constant companions, and Popo, my four-legged child, who left me the day I submitted the manuscript. My acknowledgement would be incomplete without mentioning Dev, who made me change many parts of the text time and again with his in-depth knowledge on digital references. Punu, your laptop saved me when mine crashed, so thank you.

Nabin Bhai and Ranjan Bhai, you were storehouses of information.

I appreciate Odisha Television Limited for providing me with rare video clippings and file photos from their archives.

Last but not the least, I am thankful to the Information and Public Relations Department of the Government of Odisha for letting me scout through their photo archives.

Index

Adivasi, 12, 21, 23, 29, 51, 54, 61, 70, 71, 73, 77, 91, 93, 94, 95, 96, 97, 108, 118, 122, 123, 132, 133, 134, 144, 186, 191, 196, 197, 219, 222, 227, 229, 230, 232
Amrit Kaal, 33, 209, 235
Azadi Ka Amrit Kaal, 33
Azadi Ka Amrit Mahotsav, 23, 24, 193

Bank of India, 7, 29, 81, 83, 84, 85, 86, 156, 176
Baripada, 1, 34, 51, 59, 84, 127, 227, 231, 232
Behera, Basudev, 43, 44
Bharatiya Janata Party (BJP), x, 2, 3, 4, 5, 6, 8, 10, 11, 13, 14, 15, 16, 17, 18, 19, 21, 23, 27, 28, 30, 32, 34, 48, 61, 71, 72, 77, 83, 92, 93, 94, 95, 96, 98, 99, 100, 103, 104, 105, 106, 107, 113, 119, 120, 122, 125, 127, 129, 130, 133, 134, 136, 149, 151, 153, 154, 159, 160, 162, 169, 185, 186, 187, 191, 192, 194, 195, 197, 214, 225, 227, 228, 229
Bhubaneswar, 1, 4, 6, 8, 13, 26, 29, 30, 34, 39, 46, 49, 50, 53, 54, 56, 59, 64, 66, 67, 70, 74, 77, 78, 79, 81, 82, 83, 84, 88, 91, 94, 113, 115, 116, 125, 137, 138, 143, 177, 178, 179, 181, 200, 201, 202, 217, 220, 228
Biju Janata Dal (BJD), x, 9, 13, 14, 15, 34, 48, 61, 71, 72, 77, 78, 93, 104, 105, 106, 107, 113, 122, 123, 125, 126, 127, 128, 129, 130, 135, 225, 228, 229, 232
BJD–BJP alliance, 34, 48, 77, 106, 122, 225
Brahma Kumaris (BKs), 140, 141, 142, 144, 145, 146, 147, 149, 203, 204, 206, 207

Chota Nagpur Tenancy (CNT) Act, 1908, 158, 159, 162

Das, Raghubar, 159, 160, 161, 166, 175, 181, 184, 197, 229, 230
Das, Rajkishore, 61, 93, 96, 100, 122, 228

Eighth Schedule to the Constitution, 133

female infanticide, 206, 209
first citizen, xi, 23, 33, 42, 62, 208

G20, 233, 234, 236
Giri, Basanta Kumar, 42, 43
Gochchayat, Chinmayee, 52, 54,

55, 57, 224
Gochchayat, Shantilata, 52, 56, 58
Gochchayat, Tanmayee, 52, 55, 56
Government Girls High School, Unit 2, 30, 50, 64

Independence, xiii, 2, 23, 24, 40, 54, 66, 189, 190, 233

Jaher, 6, 35, 38, 78, 111, 199
jal, jungle aur jameen, 39, 119, 160, 194, 230
Jharkhand, x, 1, 2, 3, 4, 9, 13, 17, 18, 29, 30, 31, 34, 35, 38, 43, 47, 59, 60, 61, 69, 89, 92, 95, 99, 104, 114, 118, 119, 131, 132, 149, 150, 151, 152, 153, 158, 159, 161, 162, 163, 165, 166, 167, 169, 170, 171, 172, 173, 174, 175, 180, 181, 183, 184, 186, 187, 188, 192, 194, 196, 197, 199, 204, 205, 213, 215, 217, 219, 221, 227, 229, 232
Jharkhand Mukti Morcha (JMM), 9, 10, 21, 25, 95, 99, 120, 123, 127, 129, 133, 162, 185, 186
Johar, 189

Kaduani Chhak, 34, 48, 51, 111
Kasturba Gandhi Balika Vidyalaya (KGBV), 170, 171, 172
Kuntala Kumari Sabat Hostel, 51

Majhi, Kartik, 50, 60, 94
Majhi, Naba, 6, 231

Mandal, Tapati, 46, 47, 48, 49, 73
Mayurbhanj, ix, 5, 34, 35, 57, 60, 61, 73, 93, 94, 117, 123, 127, 128, 129, 131, 136, 137, 150, 160, 176, 198, 214, 229, 232, 238
Middle English (ME) School, 43
Mishra, Ishwar Chandra, 7, 156, 176, 203
Modi, Narendra, 3, 6, 9, 10, 11, 12, 15, 21, 23, 24, 33, 75, 135, 178, 190, 192, 193
Mohanta, Chotulal, 107, 130
Mohanta, Rabindra Nath, 93, 103
Mohanto, Bikash Chandra, 2, 151
Moquim, Mohammed, 19, 20
motherland, 48, 156, 216, 233
mother tongue, 48, 130, 131, 135, 216, 217, 218, 219, 220, 234
Murmu, Dangi, 7, 52, 225
Murmu, Itishree, 5, 157
Murmu, Laxman, 137, 138, 154
Murmu, Pandit Raghunath, 35, 78, 131, 132
Murmu, Shyam Charan, 7, 79, 80, 81, 82, 83, 84, 85, 87, 93, 95, 96, 97, 101, 127, 142, 143, 144, 154, 156, 176
Murmu, Sipun, 142, 154

Nadda, J.P., 3, 4, 10, 16
National Commission for Scheduled Tribes, 159, 192
National Democratic Alliance (NDA), 2, 3, 5, 6, 8, 9, 10, 12, 17, 18, 19, 20, 21, 24, 33, 120,

Index

152, 163, 192, 198
Notified Area Council (NAC), x, 72, 94, 96, 99, 100, 101, 102, 103, 229

Odisha, ix, x, xiii, 1, 2, 6, 8, 9, 10, 13, 14, 15, 16, 19, 20, 21, 23, 24, 29, 30, 31, 34, 35, 36, 38, 54, 59, 60, 64, 65, 69, 71, 72, 75, 77, 78, 93, 104, 105, 107, 119, 122, 123, 125, 126, 127, 131, 132, 133, 136, 143, 153, 155, 158, 164, 176, 178, 191, 197, 205, 210, 212, 217, 219, 220, 221, 223, 225, 238
Ol Chiki, 35, 78, 131, 133, 134, 135

Padhy, Surama, 30, 71, 124, 143, 214, 220
Pahadpur, 5, 26, 80, 82, 83, 154, 155, 177
Parliament, xiii, xiv, 8, 10, 12, 15, 16, 22, 162, 188, 189, 227, 235, 236
Patel, Ranjan, 153, 181, 185, 197
Pathalgadi movement, 163
Patnaik, Aditya, 117, 118
Patnaik, Naveen, 8, 9, 14, 15, 24, 48, 78, 106, 107, 109, 111, 114, 119, 121, 127, 132, 191, 220
Patnaik, Rabindra, 29, 30, 85, 144
PESA Act of 1996, 159
Poonawala, Shehzaad, 192
Pradhan, Dharmendra, 14, 24, 41, 220, 224
Purty, Prahlad, 25, 185
Putti, 39, 78, 190

Rairangpur, x, 1, 2, 4, 6, 26, 27, 28, 29, 30, 47, 49, 50, 60, 61, 62, 72, 80, 83, 84, 85, 88, 93, 94, 95, 99, 100, 101, 102, 103, 104, 105, 107, 109, 110, 120, 123, 128, 130, 134, 137, 141, 142, 143, 144, 146, 149, 150, 151, 152, 153, 154, 177, 180, 181, 185, 186, 201, 202, 204, 214, 229, 231
Raj Bhavan, 43, 59, 78, 107, 159, 163, 166, 179, 180, 181, 183, 185, 223
Raj Yoga, 140, 141, 145, 147
Rama Devi Choudhury, 30, 54, 56, 64, 65, 66, 67, 219, 223
Rama Devi Women's University, 30, 56, 64, 65, 66, 67
Ram, Nabin Kumar, 6, 83, 92, 94, 96, 99, 115, 160, 195
Rashtrapati Bhavan, 33, 43, 56, 78, 173, 180, 186, 199, 215, 225, 226, 230
Reddy, Pragnya, 208, 209
Rising India through Spiritual Empowerment (RISE), 206, 207

Samal, Satish Chandra, 110, 115
Santal, 6, 35, 36, 37, 39, 57, 97, 131, 132, 175, 182
Santali, ix, 25, 35, 36, 75, 77, 78, 81, 130, 131, 132, 133, 134, 135, 185, 186, 197, 203, 229
Santhal Pargana Tenancy (SPT) Act, 1949, 158, 159, 162
Saraswati, Swami Lakshmananda, 125
sattwik, 146, 181, 185
Shyam, Laxman, Sipun (SLS)

Memorial Residential School, 154, 156, 177
Similipal Tiger Reserve, 128
Singo, 39, 84
Sinha, Yashwant, 11, 19, 21, 32, 33
Soren, Delha, 71, 73, 79, 117, 138, 180
Soren, Shibu, 9, 10, 13
spirituality, 138, 142
Sri Aurobindo Integral Education and Research Centre, 29, 85, 87, 147

tribal welfare, 61, 158
Tudu, Bhagat, 26, 84
Tudu, Biranchi Narayan, 39, 80, 81
Tudu, Dulari, 26, 27, 62, 84
Tudu, Jyotirmayee, 36, 197
Tudu, Sakramani, 29, 80, 180
Tudu, Taranisen, 29, 80, 149

United Commercial (UCO) Bank, 150, 200
University Lok Adalat, 165, 166, 167, 168, 169
Uparbeda, 1, 25, 27, 34, 35, 38, 39, 40, 42, 43, 47, 48, 49, 50, 60, 61, 80, 84, 111, 118, 137, 176, 177, 202, 223, 231
Uparbeda Government Upper Primary School, 40

vasudhaiva kutumbakam, 216, 233

women's education, 75
women's empowerment, 24, 76, 203, 205, 208

Yadav, Neera, 169